UNLEASH YOUR INNER GODDESS

The Art Of Empowered Dressing

MARY GRANT

JOURNEY INK PUBLISHING
COLORADO, USA

Journey Ink Publishing
An imprint of Journey Institute Press,
a division of 50 in 52 Journey, Inc.

journeyinstitutepress.org

Library of Congress Control Number: 2023949965

Names: Grant, Mary

Title: Unleash Your Inner Goddess

Description: Colorado: Journey Ink Publishing, 2024

Identifiers: ISBN 979-8-9894379-0-0 (hardcover)

I979-8-9894379-7-9 (paperback) 979-8-9894379-8-6 (eook / kindle)

Subjects: BISAC: SELF-HELP / Fashion & Style |

BODY, MIND & SPIRIT /Inspiration & Personal Growth

BUSINESS & ECONOMICS / Women in Business |

First Edition

Printed in the United States of America I 2 3 4 5 2I33 42 55 26

This book was typeset in Trajan Pro 3 / Cormorant Garamond

What if your wardrobe was a mindset toolkit that empowered you to step out of your bedroom every morning . . . ready to conquer the world?

CONTENTS

EMBRACE YOUR BODY SHAPE

THE POWER OF COLOUR

CURATE YOUR PERSONAL STYLE

PREFACE

It was the week of my fortieth birthday. As I stood in front of my closet, I felt lost. Even though I had a closet full of designer clothes, there was *nothing* I wanted to wear.

For the previous ten years, I had been living on autopilot.

My identity had gone AWOL.

Who was this woman looking back at me from the mirror? I had no idea who she was, what she wanted in life, who she wanted to be, or where she was going.

I felt old, frumpy, irrelevant, and well and truly stuck. It was the worst feeling ever, trumping the messy divorce I had survived and the challenges I faced as I juggled single parenting with building my business between school runs. To add insult to injury, I was a fashion designer. It was my purpose in life to make women feel great every day, how the heck had I ended up in this place myself?

My wardrobe was an accurate representation of everything I was feeling. It was a mishmash of everything I had experienced in my life over the previous twenty years. Most of what I was looking at was rarely worn. There were pieces that belonged to a different chapter of my life, buying mistakes with the labels still on, not to mention the various sizes that didn't fit, which were just a constant reminder of the body I had before I had kids. So, I gutted that closet and started from scratch, piecing it and myself back together bit by bit. It was a journey that took me over six months, as I first had to figure out who I was and what version of me I needed to take to this new decade of my life.

Only then could I decide how I wanted to show up in the world.

When I finally got back on track, I promised myself this would never happen again. I also vowed to find a way to help other women get and *stay* unstuck too.

It took several years for me to get around to writing my first #1 bestselling book, *Empowered by Style*, in 2019. Since then, I have been creating coaching programmes around the content of the book with insights from my coaching clients.

These women have helped me dial in my process for helping women evolve effortlessly from one chapter of life to another, showing up powerfully as the most authentic version of themselves, ready to take on and conquer every day.

This book is a revision of my first book. Instead of giving you more words, I wanted to pare back the fluff and give you the mindset shifts that create transformation and keep you evolving over time.

Your wardrobe can be a powerful mindset toolkit. It can help you reflect who you authentically are onto how you show up in the world. It can help you embody the best version of YOU with the precise mindset for every situation. It can help you how up powerfully every day as the right version of YOU to crush the day ahead . . . in the same time as it takes you to throw on a pair of jeans and a hoodie.

This book will show you how to use the Style Archetype Formula to curate a personal style that is authentic, empowering, and effortless and that evolves with you over time.

INTRODUCTION

THE BACK STORY

A creative upbringing laid the foundation for my journey in the fashion world which began in 1993. My parents were the epitome of creativity in their own right. My mum always had my siblings and I in matching outfits, and she used to make doll's house furniture out of matchboxes. She's in her eighties now and still spends her time yarn bombing. My dad is a DIY enthusiast and a skilled woodturner. Today we share a passion for photography and regularly attend events together.

I never had any grand notions about being a fashion designer. I went to college to learn how to make patterns. I had a dream of working from home, so if I ever had kids, I could be with them while doing something I loved.

But something changed when I stepped into that college classroom. It was the first time I remember really levelling up. Sure, my sketches might have resembled chicken scratch, and my preferred design method involved fabric and scissors, but I soon realised I had a knack for turning nothing into something unique.

As I ventured further into the fashion world, I explored every facet of personal style. As my creative journey took me through various milestones and experiences, each phase of my life reflected in my designs. Buyers at boutiques often joked that they could tell what was happening in my life by looking at my collections. I've had the privilege of curating collections and editorial photoshoots that have touched upon every style archetype in this book, mastering the art of combining and evolving them over time.

My thirty years in the fashion industry have been one long adventure with plenty of ups and downs. Three small kids and a divorce later, and I was levelling up again. This time I had to get serious about making money so I could keep a roof over our heads and educate the most important people in my life.

It has been a twisty road full of adventure, from winning awards to wholesaling to high-end boutiques, to five years in Ireland's premium department store, to pop-ups that broke sales records, to opening and running my own stores. It has also been a tale of near misses, leaky financial buckets, and trusting the wrong people, which took me to the edge of the cliff on a few occasions. Somehow, as I was teetering on the edge, I always managed to pivot and find a new direction. But there was an invisible thread connecting all the adventures that was unintentional and unconscious until that horrible big 4-0 crisis.

I always had an element of my business that kept me in direct contact with my customers. For many years, that was a studio in my house. On Saturday mornings, my team would open the door to find people sitting on our front step who had travelled from all over the country. They often brought their kids, who played with mine in the back garden. It was so much fun for all. Kids were happy. Mums got to play dress up. I got first-hand feedback that fed into my design. But the best part that I didn't recognise until many years later was the conversations. I've always been somebody that people share their secrets with. My best friends from childhood joke that if you committed murder, I would be the only person you could tell where you hid the body. Sorry if that's a bit out there, but I always found it amusing, and it is very accurate. I'm the best keeper of secrets. So, people shared a lot with me.

I got to hear about all the things women struggle with that get them stuck in life and in their heads. (Just to share one of the statistics from my coaching, 95 per cent of the women who have taken my Aligned for Success Scorecard said that they get stuck in life and in their heads. So, if you can relate, you are in good company!) Having and raising kids, changing body shapes, milestone birthdays, new chapters, pivots in our career, divorce, second marriages, illness, loss, empty nests . . . the list of curveballs and places that can get us stuck is endless.

When I was designing, I would see the faces of my customers. They were my muses. I had a mental checklist that I ran every piece through to make sure it was ticking all the boxes for my customers to ensure that when they put my pieces on, they just felt fabulous without even knowing why. It was all in the cut and in the fabric.

My design process has always started with the fabrics. They have to feel amazing next to the skin. They are all sourced in Europe, mostly from Italy (the Italians do it like nobody else can).

My collections are designed to last not for years but for decades and have been passed down from one generation to the next.

But, over time, designing wasn't enough for me anymore. I had a burning desire to have more impact in the world. I wanted to serve my customers on a much deeper level, but I was caught in the cycle of the fashion seasons, and it seemed like there was no way out.

Then Covid happened. I closed my stores for two weeks, and you know how that story goes! In the moment, I thought this was the cliff I couldn't step away from. Finally, my business was going to hurtle over the edge and there was nothing I could do about it.

So resigned to our fate, my daughter (who is my brand manager) and I decided we were just going to take the opportunity to enjoy the time together and figure out the shitshow along with everyone else. Over the following months, we showed up on social media just sharing our silly moments. People told us we were the highlight of their day, and suddenly our website was clocking sales daily. Figuring it out as I went along, I decided not to reopen our stores and focused instead on reducing the size of my collections and implementing a new business model.

I would now release capsule collections and release them at times that made sense with the seasonal changes in the weather. My capsule collections are designed so people can add one or two pieces each season to expand their outfit options and build their personal capsule over many years.

But the best part about the Covid times was I had just started a coaching diploma when Covid hit. Now I had time to follow that desire for a more meaningful impact.

In my coaching, I work with purpose-driven entrepreneurs and leaders. These women often don't have time to spend thinking about what to wear. I know, it's ironic; I have been a designer for thirty years and even I do not want to spend my time thinking about what to wear. But, like every other woman I know, I do like to look and feel good. I just want it to be effortless!

That's the beauty of the Style Archetype Formula – you curate a collection of pieces that serve you every day, and you just grab and go, knowing that you don't have to second-guess yourself.

And a sneak peek into what awaits in this book: by the end, you'll not only redefine how you approach your day but also discover the three mindsets that empower you in every aspect of life. You'll match these mindsets with an archetype that resonates with you, building outfits where everything just works together.

No more shopping mistakes or wardrobe waste.

You'll become the gatekeeper of your closet, ensuring that every piece takes you intentionally in the direction you desire.

HOW TO USE THIS BOOK

This book is not an instruction manual.

It's written to inspire you to think about how you can use your desired mindsets in different areas of your life to inform how you curate your closet.

The focus here is to help women show up powerfully and evolve effortlessly in different areas and chapters of life.

Section 1: Unleash Your Inner Goddess

When I say the words "inner goddess" to women, they often respond with, "Who, me?" Most women think this description fits others, but not them.

This is the first mindset shift we'll explore.

Section 2: The Style Archetype Formula

In this section, I'll start by explaining what the archetypes are, and why they exist.

We'll walk through the three groups of archetypes, each containing three archetypes, for a total of nine archetypes. Come to this with an open mind. These archetypes are not meant to pigeonhole you, but to provide you with a toolkit to curate the most authentic version of yourself.

Each archetype comes with an inspirational list that can help you identify your most authentic archetypes and eliminate future shopping mistakes. You'll also have the opportunity to take the Style Archetype Quiz to determine your main archetype.

Section 3: Embrace Your Body Shape

Personal style is intimately tied to body shape. We'll delve into the five main body shapes, helping you identify which one best represents you. This section will provide a list of things to try for your specific body shape.

Section 4: The Power of Colour

Understanding colour is key to defining your personal style. In this section, we'll explore two aspects of colour:

1. Discover which colour palette resonates with you, to build your wardrobe around.

2. Explore colour psychology to understand how different colours can not only enhance your mood and outcomes, but also influence other people's perceptions and reactions.

Section 5: Curate Your Personal Style

In this section, I will raise awareness of the most common mistakes and limiting beliefs I have observed around personal style. Some people are totally unaware of them until they hear them, and then they seem glaringly obvious.

I will explain the difference between different wardrobe-building styles that you may have heard of so you can adapt one that best suits you.

Then I will introduce you to the CURATE Framework—a memorable tool I created just for this book, to maximise your wardrobe, maintain focus during planning and shopping, and save you a fortune over time.

UNLEASH YOUR INNER GODDESS

CHAPTER 1

EVERY WOMAN'S
CLOSET TELLS A STORY

Every woman's closet tells a story of who she is, where she's headed, the journey she's embraced, and the challenges that have shaped who she is today.

Every woman's closet tells the story of what she believes to be true about herself and how the world sees her.

But lurking behind those closet doors are pieces that do not serve her: clothes that do not fit; jeans in several different sizes; memories of eras past, never to be revisited; impulse buys; and outfits bought for special occasions that never see the light of day.

Too often, when a woman throws open her closet doors looking for inspiration, instead she is greeted by frustration.

But what if your wardrobe offered more than just a collection of garments? What if it could reflect your inner essence ... be your source of empowerment, the catalyst of your life's transformation?

Welcome to the Style Archetype Formula. You are stepping into an adventure not just of creating your personal style, but of personal transformation. Between the covers of this book is your secret formula for creating a mindset toolkit using something you have in common with every other woman you know . . . your clothes.

Your clothes are the most underutilised tool in your arsenal for showing up as the right version of you for every occasion, whether that's levelling up for an audacious business goal, morphing into exactly the right version of you for a date night, or revving up to power through a to-do list.

My journey spans over three decades of designing clothes and engaging in countless conversations with women just like you. Yet, our conversations were rarely about clothes; they delved into life's essence—its challenges, joys, and the incredible strength that rises to the surface in a woman as she juggles life's challenges while caring for the people who mean the most to her.

Your style transcends clothing; it's a manifestation of how you enter a room, claim your space, and conquer your world. The enchantment here is that you don't need to be pigeonholed or confined to rules. It's time to open doors, dissolve boundaries, and feel empowered to embrace your authentic self.

The Style Archetype Formula is not just a title; it's your guide to unleashing your inner goddess.

These archetypes? They aren't mere categories; they're gateways to distinct mindsets that you can embrace as comfortably as your favourite pair of jeans.

The archetypes are your building blocks, and you're the creator. A touch of this, a splash of that, and voilà! Your personal style is ready to shine. And we won't overlook how body shapes and colour palettes can enhance your individuality.

Crafting a captivating style isn't about overwhelming choices; it's about discovering what aligns naturally with you. It's about identifying the perfect choices for you so you can ditch buying mistakes forever.

No more wrestling with trends that don't resonate or trying to fit into outfits that don't reflect the authentic you, no matter what the occasion.

Get ready to unleash timeless self-expression–empowered dressing that's profoundly personal and effortlessly put together.

CHAPTER 2

UNLEASH YOUR INNER GODDESS

Let's dive into the heart of it all – your inner goddess. This isn't about mythology or ancient stories; it's about the fierce and fabulous you.

Discovering Your Inner Goddess

You know that feeling when you slip into an outfit that just makes you feel like . . . well, you? That's your inner goddess shining through. It's that confident, radiant version of yourself that deserves to step into the spotlight every single day.

Empowering Your True Self

Believe it or not, the clothes you choose in the morning hold immense power. They're not just fabrics, a means to cover your body; they're a statement. When you pick an outfit that resonates with your inner essence, something magical happens. Your posture changes, your smile becomes brighter, and you radiate a newfound aura of confidence.

And guess what?

It doesn't just affect you–everyone around you benefits from this positive energy.

Self-Confidence: Your Stylish Ally

Let's be real–we all have days when we doubt ourselves. But the right outfit can be your secret weapon against self-doubt. It's like your own personal cheerleader, reminding you of your worth, strength, and beauty. It's not about conforming to someone else's standards, rather celebrating who you are.

Unveiling Your Authenticity

You might be wondering, "Can I really be authentically me and ditch trends or the expectations of others?"

You absolutely can!

When you curate your personal style to be a physical extension of who you authentically are, you show up in the world powerfully, and this sends a clear message and a lasting impression. You *can* curate a uniform, a way you show up and when it is consistent, that people come to know you for. It's like your personal statement about who you are and where you are going in life.

It's all about finding the balance between expressing yourself and navigating the world around you so you show up as the right version of you for each area of life. Remember, your style should feel like a second skin–comfortable, natural, and uniquely yours.

In a world where society makes assumptions about women based on their appearance, your personal style becomes a powerful tool for self-expression. It's not about being a fashion icon but being unapologetically you. It's about using your clothing as your armour of confidence and authenticity.

CHAPTER 3

THE ART OF EMPOWERED DRESSING

I t all starts within.

Creating your authentic style is a form of self-mastery. You cannot achieve it without having first assessed who you are, what you like, and how you want to show up in the world.

It is never too early or too late to develop or change direction with your personal style. Whenever you do, you will be free of trends and other people's expectations forever. You will be clearer about who you are and what you stand for, and you will be more confident in your inner world, which is reflected in your outer world. What you wear every day can influence every aspect of your life. After all, this is the first thing that people see when they meet you, and while we shouldn't judge a book by the cover, the reality is that we do. Even if you are not meeting people, you judge yourself when you look in the mirror. Am I right? Put the thought and preparation into what you want your appearance to say and watch how you can make things happen.

This process involves putting a little bit of work in now, then regularly revisiting, so you evolve effortlessly as you go through life. You don't have to have a tonne of clothes to have style; you can have a very distinctive style with surprisingly few pieces. Style is more about attitude than affluence.

When you develop your style, it sends a message to the world that says you know who you are and where you are going.

Unapologetically You

Showing up as your most authentic self has many well-being and mindset benefits.

Invest in yourself

Taking the time to develop your personal style gives you a feeling of self-worth, which can spread to other areas as you become more curious about how else you can invest in yourself. It's like an energy that breeds more energy, taking you to other places of personal growth that you never imagined. When I started to become more strategic in how I showed up, I gained clarity, headspace, and focus. The right version of me, showing up with the right mindset in every situation, cleared the way for all kinds of opportunities.

Feel more confident

Being conscious of the clothes that suit you and being able to reassess and quickly adapt as your body changes throughout life gives you a huge confidence boost and will stop you getting stuck in a negative headspace. It will also prevent you from buying things that do not work for you. You won't buy clothes for the person that you once were or the person that you hope to be in six months' time. You will dress for who you are today, making the best of your assets. Any changes, like losing weight, are a bonus down the road, but you can still sparkle while you are getting there. Don't wait until "X" happens before you give yourself permission to be fabulous. You are fabulous *exactly* the way you are.

Create more time

When you develop your own personal style, you are more decisive when shopping. You will know what works and what doesn't. There will be less going back and forth making exchanges, and you will crave fewer shopping trips, leaving more time for all the other fun things in life!

You will also spend less time thinking about what to wear and less time getting dressed! That's a whole lot of extra time and headspace, which is, after all, what we crave most as busy women.

Improve your mood

We all have days when we wake up in a bad mood. These are the days that we need to make the most effort.

These are the days when stepping out of your bedroom as the most empowered version of you will instantly up-level your day.

I promise you, this doesn't have to take long. Simple rituals that you can implement in less than five minutes will do the job nicely . . . like planning your outfit the night before and having a simple makeup regime for during the week, even if that is just mascara and lip gloss.

Be more comfortable

The thinking involved in developing your own style will ensure that you have a wardrobe full of comfortable things. You will eliminate mistakes that end up sitting on the rail. How many times have you pushed away items that you have to fix all day long in search of a more effortless, comfortable option? When you are constantly assessing and evolving, these items will never make it into your closet. (Pay close attention to your footwear in this respect.)

Spend more wisely

When you know exactly what works for you and why, you will buy less, which allows you to buy better. Investment pieces that you previously lusted after suddenly feel like the only option.

Quality items that you absolutely love, well cared for, will last for years. Think of these in terms of value per wear. Compare these investment pieces to cheaper items that do nothing to inspire or empower you and just don't last. The cheaper pieces cost you more in the long run.

Be in control

Curating and using your wardrobe as a mindset toolkit ensures you step out of your bedroom every morning ready to conquer the day. You are already winning. That mindset brings more of the same throughout the day.

Showing up powerfully helps you take on life's challenges fearlessly. You will feel more in control of your destiny, and people will think twice about crossing you!

Being your most confident self allows you to become non-reactive to situations, which instils confidence in the people around you. They know they can rely on you in a crisis. This is invaluable in all situations.

Reap the rewards

As with everything, you reap what you sow. When you put the work in, you will be effortlessly fabulous. You will enjoy getting dressed because you know that no matter what you put your hand on in your wardrobe, it will just work for you, and you will have several options for how you wear it.

You will start the day comfortable and inspired. You will have a more positive body image because you know you have put in the work, choosing pieces because they work for you.

You will be your most authentic self. When those around you know that you have a distinct style that is yours, they are less inclined to tell you what you should wear.

Nobody should be allowed to dictate to you how to dress, not even on special occasions. You will remain true to yourself, and other people will realise that this is non-negotiable.

THE STYLE ARCHETYPE FORMULA

CHAPTER 4

THE ESSENCE OF STYLE ARCHETYPES

So, what exactly are style archetypes?

The style archetypes are a unique concept in the world of personal style. They provide a framework of distinct personas. Think of an archetype as an avatar, a distinct character with its own personality, characteristics, and fashion preferences.

The reason the archetypes are so effective is that it's easier to see the characteristics of a personality when you're not trying to apply it to yourself.

By exploring the archetypes, you can gain valuable insights into their personal style and use them as a toolkit to curate a wardrobe that truly reflects your authentic self.

As you are working your way through this section, stop and think of the people you know and try to guess what their archetype is. This is a fun exercise that helps you to dial in your own archetype.

The Birth of the Style Archetypes

As I mentioned already, in the past three decades of running my fashion business, I've always enjoyed getting to know my customers. I never wanted to chat about clothes, so I always steered our conversations towards life's ups and downs, the real stuff.

I also mentioned that I've seen all the places in life where women get stuck. Over time, it became my burning desire to help women get and stay unstuck so they can go further and fly higher in life. We just don't need life's curveballs slowing us down.

Then, one day, as I was casually flipping through the Myers–Briggs personality types, something incredible happened. I had an "a-ha!" moment. It was as if a light bulb went off. I suddenly realised that I could see my customers' faces in these personality types, and it hit me that there was a striking consistency in how these different personalities showed up in the world.

So, I printed out those personality types, literally cut them into pieces, and scattered them across my kitchen table. It was like the pieces of a puzzle coming together. I could clearly see that these personality types neatly fell into nine archetypes across three overarching categories. Each category had an overarching mindset and each archetype its unique style personality. It was like they were just sitting there waiting to be discovered and I had just tripped right over them!

When you pick one archetype from each of these three categories and blend them together, you've got yourself a mindset toolkit. This toolkit works wonders in curating your closet so that you effortlessly show up for any occasion, no sweat.

Unleashing Your Authenticity

The Style Archetype Formula isn't just about choosing outfits—it's about connecting who you authentically are with how you show up in the world and bringing the right mindset to every occasion.

This is a journey of self-discovery and transformation that comes along for the ride while you are curating and evolving your personal style.

Imagine opening your closet each morning and feeling a connection with every piece of clothing. Each item, colour, and accessory adds to your unique style. Your wardrobe isn't just about clothes—it's a way to express your strength, vulnerabilities, dreams, and authenticity.

Get ready to embrace your archetypes and take on the world with confidence—one outfit at a time.

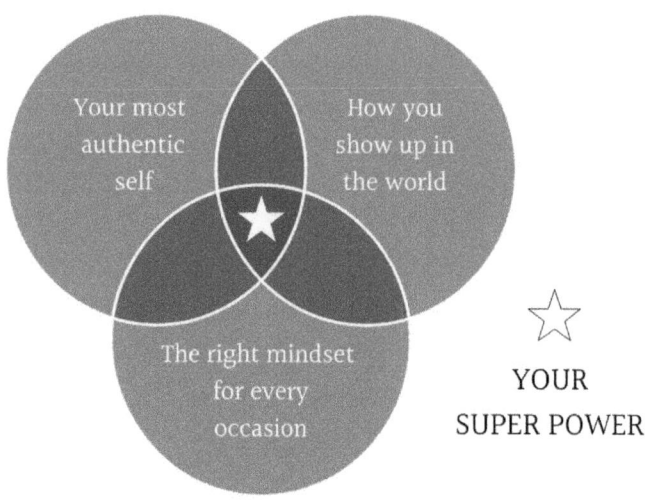

YOUR
SUPER POWER

Your Style Archetype Toolkit

Your leading lady

Everyone has one main style archetype that they gravitate towards.

The pieces that are already in your closet that make you feel amazing and most like yourself when you wear them point you towards your main archetype. I like to call her your leading lady.

In a few minutes, I will get you to take the Style Archetype Quiz, which will reveal which archetype is your leading lady. First, I want to tell you why knowing this is not enough.

Your secondary archetypes

The first step on this journey is identifying your "leading lady." The second is choosing two archetypes who support her.

Here's why.

Remember I mentioned that each archetype has an overarching mindset? Well, your leading lady will naturally fall into one of these three main groups. But, as you know, one version of you is not right in every situation and area of life. Different situations require different versions of you.

The version of you who shows up for an important business meeting is not the version you want to take to a relaxed family day . . . different mindset required, right?

The version of you that you take to meet a friend for lunch is not the version that will power through a to-do list . . . This version of you won't help you get any work done.

The soft, feminine version of you may struggle to assert herself, but adding a bit of badass to your wardrobe when you need to be taken seriously will send a clear "don't f*** with me" message to the world.

The version of you who is ready for a chill-out day probably won't serve you well when you want to clarify your future vision or next-level strategies.

The good news is that you can curate a version of you that is perfect for any situation using only three archetypes.

When you use the style archetypes, you can create your mindset toolkit for every situation using outfit choices you can have on standby for every situation. This means you don't have to be constantly thinking about what to wear.

Remember, these archetypes are not there to put you in a box or limit your creativity. They're like a lens that helps you better see different parts of yourself. Maybe you're a Creative who loves expressing yourself, a Romantic who brings softness and allure, or a Trail Blazer who challenges norms. These archetypes help you embrace different sides of yourself while building a personal style that makes you feel strong and confident.

A side note before we dive in . . .

You can aspire to any archetype, especially if you seek change. Start with a few key pieces and build your collection gradually. Successful archetype combinations require practice, so try them out privately first. Avoid adopting an archetype solely for special occasions, as it can feel uncomfortable. Understand each archetype's personality traits to influence your mindset.

Pay attention to what resonates with you and what doesn't; this helps eliminate buying mistakes. Be mindful that your current reality may differ from your aspirations. Start where you are now, make sustainable changes, and add to them over time. Begin with the easy wins, like updating hair, makeup, and accessories, which can instantly refresh your look and boost your confidence.

OK, that said, let's dive in . . .

CHAPTER 5

THE STYLE ARCHETYPE QUIZ

B efore we move on to exploring the different archetypes, take a moment to do the Style Archetype Quiz.

Hundreds of women like you have taken the quiz over the last four years. Because of its accuracy, it has never been necessary to change the questions.

Remember, there are no hard and fast rules. Your leading lady will show up nine times out of ten, but sometimes one of your supporting role archetypes will show up. It all depends on the day and what is going on for you, so feel free to take the quiz as many times as you want.

www.stylearchetypequiz.com

CHAPTER 6

THE THINKER ARCHETYPES

THE SOPHISTICATE
THE TRAIL BLAZER
THE MINIMALIST

"I kept getting the Trail Blazer when I was doing the quiz. I wasn't sure if it was the right result for me until Mary said, 'Pay attention to the details.' Suddenly it all made sense. Knowing my archetype has helped me to spot the best buys for me."

– MARTHA (COACHING CLIENT)

As we start this exciting adventure, let's explore the world of the Thinkers, the Feelers, and the Do-ers

The Thinkers | The Feelers | The Do-ers

Each archetype group represents a mindset for approaching life, a unique essence that shines through your clothing choices.

The Thinker's Essence: Your Highest-Level Self

Natural Thinker archetypes thrive in leadership roles. People who are Thinkers are known to be more interested in big ideas than in mundane and practical activities.

They have a clear and identifiable no-nonsense approach to their personal style. They mix well with the Do-er archetypes for downtime and need to ensure some of their wardrobe will allow them to switch off.

Thinkers may not always understand the more touchy-feely archetype styles, but they can take influences from these archetypes to bring out their softer, more feminine side.

People whose main archetype is outside the Thinker group can tap into this group when they want to level up in any area of life or show up powerfully in challenging situations.

Remember, this is not just about the clothes; it's about embracing a mindset that puts the most powerful version of you in the driver's seat.

The Role of the Thinker Archetypes in Your Closet

The Thinker archetype supports you in enhancing your mindset when confronting significant challenges, chasing ambitious goals, or navigating life's important moments.

She's your companion for vital business meetings, important events, and formal occasions. With the Thinker archetype, you emanate intellectual strength and self-assuredness, leaving a lasting impact.

Throughout our exploration of the Thinker archetypes, remember that these mindsets go beyond specific occasions. They infuse your daily style with elements that align with your inner brilliance.

The Thinker archetypes help you embrace your intellectual strength and express it outwardly in your appearance, contributing to your confidence and empowerment.

THE TRAIL BLAZER

Signature Traits

*Forward thinking, Unique
Avant garde, Unconventional,
Inventive*

The Trail Blazer embodies the spirit of a thought leader. However, she doesn't necessarily seek recognition as one, for she pursues her own path with unwavering determination, regardless of who's watching. Known for her lightning-fast pace, she's adept at moving forward, navigating life's challenges no matter how daunting they may seem. Her distinctive style is a source of admiration among those who surround her, who often turn to her for inspiration. An out-and-out Trail Blazer exudes a futuristic vibe, sometimes manifesting in extravagant fashion choices. Her love for pushing the boundaries of convention extends to every aspect of her life.

This archetype gravitates towards shapes that are conceptual, expressive, bold, and perfect for layering, resulting in an original and edgy appearance. Unlike some other archetypes, she doesn't prioritise showcasing her body; instead, her clothing holds a deeply personal connection. The Trail Blazer is drawn to quality and unique items, cultivating one of the most individualistic wardrobes. When it comes to colour, her wardrobe can range from monochrome elegance, including blacks, whites, greys, and metallics, to bursts of vibrant and unconventional colours.

The Trail Blazer's wardrobe serves as a well of inspiration for thinking outside the box. She possesses a knack for selecting pieces that effortlessly mix and match, providing her with versatile outfit options. Evolution is second nature to her, as she continuously refines her style. However, her bold and edgy appearance may occasionally appear intimidating to those less inclined toward style consciousness. To forge connections with individuals who may not share her penchant for avant-garde fashion, she may choose to soften her look.

The Trail Blazer's preference is for an edgy yet timeless style. She opts for pieces less influenced by trends and more aligned with her distinctive personality.

Meet Donna . . .

Donna is a Trail Blazer who owns a boutique hotel. Her days are a whirlwind of meeting and greeting guests while creating top-tier customer experiences. Donna's wardrobe is a unique blend of quirky pieces she's collected over the years, which she effortlessly layers, adding her personal touch with unconventional boots and statement jewellery.

However, Donna faces several challenges common to many Trail Blazers: the need for slowing down and empowering others to step up. Being a Trail Blazer by nature means that you are always one step ahead, looking to the future and making things happen. This can leave mere mortals in the dust. To empower and connect with others who may be intimidated takes awareness and intention on the part of the Trail Blazer.

To help Donna slow down, we tapped into the Romantic archetype. A capsule of soft, tactile pieces and colours helps her unwind after hectic days and keep that head switched off when relaxing with family at the weekends. It also brings out her soft, feminine side that makes her more approachable in work situations. She also uses her Romantic archetype with intention when she knows she is going to be dealing with difficult situations.

As Donna thrives on customer interactions, she can find it hard to tie herself to her desk, so we tailored a capsule of Provider-inspired pieces to keep her focused when handling paperwork and administrative tasks. The balance across all areas helps her to show up powerfully across all areas of her life.

If you are this archetype, great secondary archetypes are . . .

The Romantic when you want to bring out your softer side and The Athlete when you want to get stuff done.

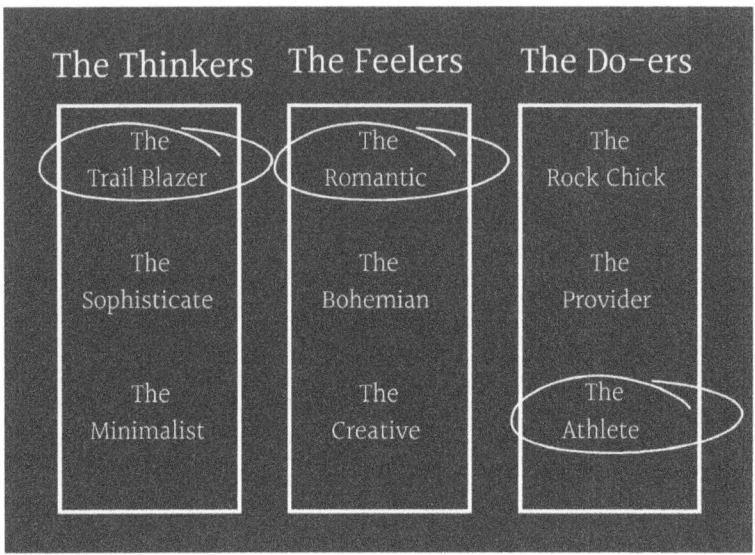

Inspiration for the Trail Blazer

✓ *Wacky coats*

✓ *Quirky jackets*

✓ *Unstructured dresses*

✓ *Avant-garde dresses*

✓ *Layering dresses*

✓ *Dramatic, iconic pieces*

✓ *Statement accessories*

✓ *Interesting textures and shapes*

✓ *Tunics*

✓ *Layering pieces*

✓ *Modern cuts*

✓ *Exaggerated ruffles and frills*

✓ *Asymmetrical hemlines*

✓ *Metallic and chunky accessories*

✓ Contrasting textures

✓ Quirky knitwear

✓ Handknits

✓ Detail: zippers, hardware, stitching, etc.

✓ Investment shoes and boots

✓ Oversized shirts

✓ Sunglasses

CHAPTER 8

THE SOPHISTICATE

Signature Traits

Sharp | Polished | Chic | Traditional | Glamorous

The Sophisticate is the embodiment of power and style. She's that person who just oozes confidence and authority, and people can't help but look up to her. When it comes to her appearance, she's all about perfection without breaking a sweat. Her clothes, hair, makeup—it's always immaculate because that's just how she rolls. She takes her career and future super seriously, and you can bet she's got her goals all mapped out.

She's got a thing for both classic and modern styles. Think sleek tailoring, clean lines, and a touch of subtle flair. You'll often spot her in well-tailored coats, dresses, and some classy, understated jewellery. What she loves most, though, are outfits that require zero brainpower to put together. She's all about simplicity, whether it's in neutrals or bold colours—as long as it's effortless, she's in.

Her closet is a practical dream for business because she's sorted her daily outfits down to a science. She doesn't let seasonal trends dictate her choices. Instead, she invests in quality classics that never go out of style. Since she's not chasing after every new fashion fad, she's got more cash to splash on items that are built to last.

But here's the deal—with her wardrobe being seasonless, she needs to remember to switch things up when the weather changes. Plus, she could do with some cosy knits or cashmere to unwind at weekends and when relaxing with friends and family. And here's a pro tip: she's got to give her feet a break from those killer heels and lighten up that handbag, both of which will deplete her energy and give her backache.

Meet Suzanne . . .

Meet Suzanne, the ultimate Sophisticate. She's the CEO of a non-profit and rocks that boardroom like a pro. Her wardrobe?

It's all about perfect tailoring and killer heels. Suzanne means business, and when she walks into a room, everyone knows it.

But here's the thing. Even a powerhouse like Suzanne needs a breather now and then, and sometimes she needs to get out of her leadership role and let somebody else take over the driver's seat. But in the past, always showing up suited and booted meant that other people never seemed to understand that and left her to be the leader in every situation. That can be exhausting, so, together we took a dive into the Romantic archetype for inspiration. Picture soft pastel colours, subtle lace trims, the occasional frill on a neckline or cuff, and cosy cashmere–it's like a stylish hug. These additions let her show a softer, nurturing side, all while blending seamlessly with her sharp suits. Because we wanted to encourage some pure self-care days to help her rejuvenate, we added some cosy cashmere-inspired jogger sets which feel like a deep sigh when she puts them on.

Suzanne's days are all about getting things done, both on an intellectual and practical level. To support her, we slipped in elements of the Provider archetype for days behind the scenes: practical, stylish pieces that keep her on top of her game. This well-rounded approach to her wardrobe lets Suzanne shift gears effortlessly between her high flyer roles, days in her office getting things done, and time off with her family where she is happy to let others take the lead – and that's good for everyone.

If you are this archetype, great secondary archetypes are . . .

The Romantic when you want to bring out your softer side. *The Provider* when you want to get stuff done. *This archetype also effortlessly mixes with elements of* **The Rock Chick** *for some badass attitude and don't forget a selection from* **The Athlete** *to inspire you to move that body.*

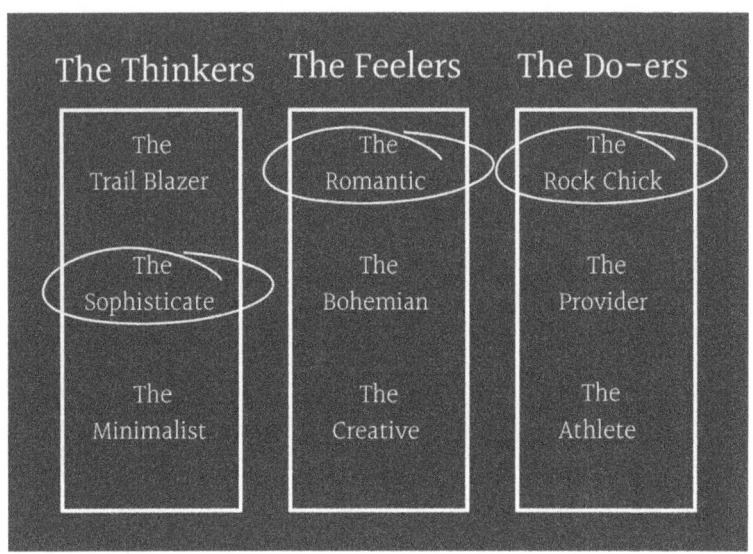

Inspiration for the Sophisticate:

- ✓ Elegant tailored coats and overcoats
- ✓ Tailored jackets
- ✓ Shift / wrap dresses
- ✓ Little black dresses
- ✓ Crew-neck sweaters
- ✓ Wrap shirts
- ✓ Simple white T-shirts

- ✓ Pencil skirts
- ✓ Skinny jeans
- ✓ Tailored trousers
- ✓ Black pumps
- ✓ Elegant flats
- ✓ Ankle boots
- ✓ Killer heels
- ✓ Classic handbags

✓ *Sunglasses*

✓ *Classic jewellery*

✓ *Assorted scarves*

✓ *Strong-colour lipstick*

CHAPTER 9

THE MINIMALIST

Signature Traits

Mindful | Timeless | Immaculate | Quality | Less is more

The Minimalist understands that a clutter-free space translates to a clutter-free mind. She's a deep thinker, constantly brewing brilliant ideas. Chaos, excess and messiness are big no-nos for her, whether in the kitchen or her closet. Her focus on grand, forward-thinking concepts means she spares little time for life's practical and mundane aspects. Even though she may not identify with being a "shopper," she's the type who will casually browse on the way to meet a friend for coffee and find the perfect pieces for her.

With an impeccable eye for detail, she values quality fabrics and mix-and-match pieces that offer a plethora of wardrobe options. Clean, uncomplicated lines are her jam, and she's drawn to multifunctional, timeless attire. Her style is all about the art of less is more–when others are piling on accessories, she's probably removing one before heading out. Neutrals are her preferred palette, easily blending and matching in her wardrobe.

Her minimalistic wardrobe is a haven for creative thinking. Simplicity creates the headspace required for those big ideas to flourish. Though she might possess fewer clothing items compared to other archetypes, the Minimalist opts for quality pieces that harmonise beautifully. Her choices are deliberate, leading to minimal waste and few fashion blunders.

However, the Minimalist can find her choices limited when it comes to special occasions. To counter this, she can ensure that her wardrobe contains a few elegant dresses or mix-and-match separates that can be elevated with statement jewellery.

The Minimalist needs to consciously refresh her wardrobe, even with minor changes. The creative mind tends to grow restless if things remain constant for too long. This archetype complements some edgier elements of the Rock Chick to maintain a sense of intrigue and can easily absorb some of the more edgy pieces or details inspired by the Trail Blazer.

Meet Maria . . .

Maria is the quintessential Minimalist and a serial entrepreneur. For her, a tidy space equals a clear mind, and this philosophy extends from her office to her kitchen to her wardrobe. Her closet is a testament to minimalism, housing timeless, well-crafted pieces within a neutral colour palette. This selection effortlessly mixes and matches, offering her a range of streamlined looks.

Maria's challenge is that she despises the kind of clothes that people sometimes expect her to wear for family occasions like weddings and evening business events, which often call for more formal wear. She would often rather not go than comply with other people's expectations. So, she intentionally added some more dressy pieces that she can mix and match with her everyday pieces. She has these covered in her closet, so she is not looking at them every day, her go-to pieces for any special occasions that arise. And here's the thing–she will wear them over and over again and not give a toss that people have seen them already.

Also, while Maria's style predominantly leans towards Minimalist, she occasionally incorporates touches of the Feeler archetypes. A few soft pink hues that blend with her neutral colour palette and delicate earrings make appearances in her wardrobe, introducing a hint of femininity and emotional depth to her otherwise pared back ensembles.

In addition to her Minimalist staples, Maria maintains a capsule of Athlete-inspired pieces like leggings, vests, and a couple of hoodies (all in black). These items seamlessly meld with her Minimalist favourites and serve as practical choices for staying active and getting things done, aligning perfectly with her dynamic entrepreneurial lifestyle.

If you are this archetype, great secondary archetypes are . . .

*The **Romantic** when you want to bring out your softer side and **The Athlete** when you want to get stuff done. Elements of **The Rock Chick** also work well for a bit of badass attitude.*

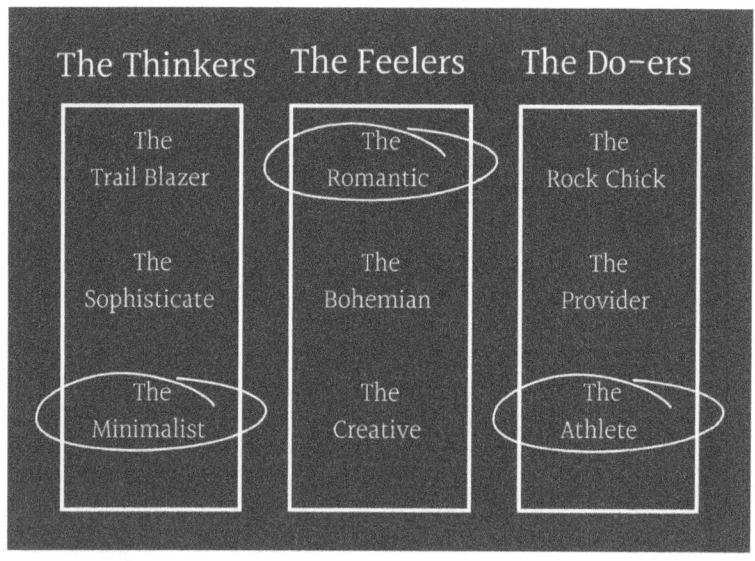

Inspiration for the Minimalist

✓ Neutral colours

✓ Clean lines and well-cut pieces

✓ Quality and natural fabrics

✓ Unstructured coats and jackets

✓ Investment knitwear and handknits

- ✓ Unstructured dresses
- ✓ Modern shapes
- ✓ Pinafores
- ✓ Layering items of every kind
- ✓ White shirts
- ✓ Jersey dresses
- ✓ T-shirts
- ✓ Skinny tops for simple layering outfits
- ✓ Cropped trousers
- ✓ Leggings
- ✓ Timeless investment shoes
- ✓ Chelsea boots, loafers, brogues
- ✓ White trainers
- ✓ Understated bags
- ✓ Simple sunglasses
- ✓ Jewellery, either simple or quirky
- ✓ Scarves

CHAPTER 10

THE FEELER ARCHETYPES

THE BOHEMIAN
THE CREATIVE
THE ROMANTIC

"Recognising that I am a Creative was life changing for me. I kept trying to buy minimalist outfits for photoshoots and be seen as 'sophisticated' for my brand. But it just wasn't working. It was actually cramping my vibrant, colourful style. So discovering the magic of

ME set me free."

– DIANE CUNNINGHAM ELLIS (BUSINESS COACH)

The Feelers' Essence: Your Heart-Centred Self

While the Thinkers help you show up as the most powerful version of yourself, the Feeler archetypes support you in showing up as the most feminine version of yourself.

Natural Feeler archetypes are warm, considerate, and nurturing. They are the intuitive members of the archetype family. The givers, carers, musicians, artists, and creators typically fall into this group. This is not to say the Feeler is a pushover; she is not. She is a strong, passionate woman who cares deeply about the well-being of the world and people in general.

These archetypes become your allies when you need to express your emotions, celebrate your femininity, and showcase your unique creativity. They are your go-to when you want to unwind, express your creativity, and be inspired.

It's not just about the clothes you wear; it's about embodying the most feminine version of yourself. This is also the archetype group to look to for inspiration when it comes to relaxing, as the softer colours and fabrics will help you slow everything down.

The Role of the Feeler Archetypes in Your Closet

As the mindset of the Feeler group embodies femininity and creativity, you are missing out on a powerful addition to your mindset toolkit if you overlook this group.

As with all of the archetypes, the addition of Feeler archetype influences will help you bring a powerful mindset to every area of your life where you want your softer, more feminine side to take the lead.

Tapping into this group of archetypes will help you navigate difficulties and conflict with better results. Think of somebody in your life who is naturally a soft, nurturing person and let them be your inspiration. As a go-getter, I have always moved at speed, but whenever I need to bring a softer version of myself to any situation, I think of my friend Lesley. I tap into my inner Lesley.

Furthermore, these archetypes support you in unwinding and exploring your creativity, adding an extra layer of depth to your style. The Feeler archetypes appreciate comfort and have interesting, soft, and often ethereal wardrobes.

Feelers can tap into the Thinker archetypes when they want to level up to a demanding situation or be taken seriously, and the Do-er group when they want to get things done.

CHAPTER 11

THE ROMANTIC

Signature Traits

Soft | Feminine | Tactile | Dreamy | Floaty

The Romantic archetype is a ray of sunshine. Whether in the frosty grip of winter or the heat of summer, the Romantic gravitates towards soft, feminine outfits that exude an air of ethereal charm. Her wardrobe is a treasure trove of flowing silhouettes, draped fabrics, and delicate lace trims that bring a sense of peace and tranquillity wherever she goes.

Generosity is her hallmark, and she thrives on giving back to others. She's all about fostering harmony and teamwork, often bringing out the best in everyone around her. With an easy-going, kind, and loving nature, she's a natural caregiver and nurturer, easily capturing the hearts of those she meets. Daydreaming is her secret pastime, and her magnetic personality makes her popular among all the other archetypes, particularly when it comes to matters of the heart.

Lace, floating fabrics, and soft pastel colours are her signature style. She may be a fan of layering chiffons, silks, and tactile jerseys, even sneaking a bit of lace into her work attire. And when she wants to add a dash of edge to her look, she turns to the Rock Chick archetype for a perfect complement.

With her often extensive wardrobe, the Romantic has a plethora of choices for downtime, special occasions, and social gatherings. Yet, because she's drawn to soft, dreamy wardrobe pieces, she needs to be intentional about curating her wardrobe to cater to all aspects of life. This strategy ensures that she can confidently step into any situation, unleashing her inner power when she wants to be taken seriously and efficiently tackling her to-do list when needs must.

Meet Sarah . . .

Sarah is a romantic at heart. She's a destination wedding planner, and her work reflects her soft, feminine essence. Her wardrobe is a romantic treasure chest, featuring soft pastel colours, floaty chiffon fabrics, and delicate lace trims. Clients are naturally drawn to her, as she effortlessly infuses every aspect of their wedding planning journey with the essence of romance.

Sarah did face a challenge in this respect. While her Romantic essence was why everyone loved her, it was confusing on the clients' actual wedding days, so Sarah had to think about how she was going to show up to be seen as the woman in charge. She did this by incorporating a Sophisticate-inspired capsule into her wardrobe. This transformation signals to everyone that she's the go-to person who makes everything run smoothly, orchestrating memorable, stress-free experiences for her clients.

There was another area in life that Sarah found challenging. Her soft, feminine nature often led people to mistakenly think that she was some kind of pushover. Sarah can take a lot, but push her too far and she will push right back. She found it stressful that she had to do this, so we injected a twist into her wardrobe, a touch of the tougher Rock Chick when she wants to send a clear message that she is not to be messed with. This is actually a lot of fun for her, as it also adds a touch of mystique to her feminine aura. Her inspiration in this respect is leather and lace. Feel free to be inspired by that!

If you are this archetype, great secondary archetypes are . . .

The Sophisticate when you want to be more business-like. The Athlete when you want to get stuff done or feel more grounded. The Rock Chick for a bit of badass attitude.

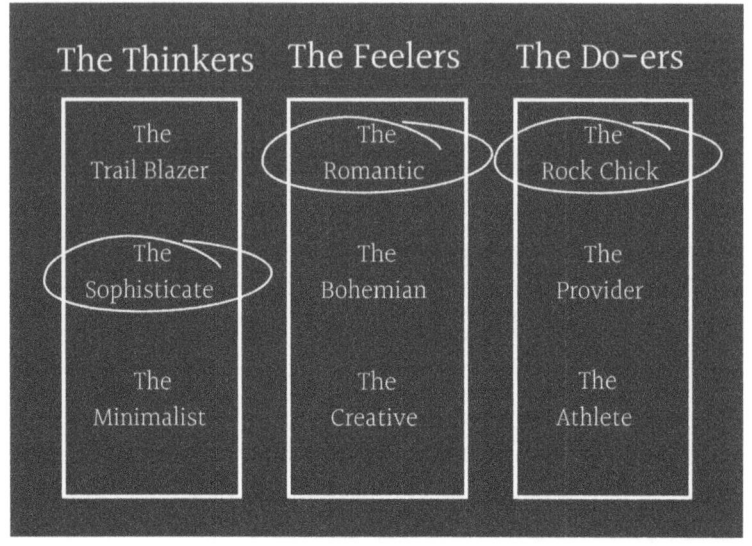

Inspirations for the Romantic

- ✓ Softly tailored coats and jackets
- ✓ Cashmere wraps
- ✓ Layered knitwear
- ✓ Oversized shirt dresses in lightweight fabrics
- ✓ Anything lace / chiffon / voile
- ✓ Soft feminine colours and prints
- ✓ All things velvet, from coats to boots
- ✓ All-white outfits
- ✓ Pretty floral prints

- ✓ Embroidery
- ✓ Unstructured shirts
- ✓ Ruffles and flounces
- ✓ Colourful shoes and sandals
- ✓ Faux fur
- ✓ Tulle
- ✓ Pretty boots and shoes
- ✓ Nude court shoes
- ✓ Layering jewellery
- ✓ Floral accessories
- ✓ Pretty hair accessories

CHAPTER 12

THE BOHEMIAN

Signature Traits

Vintage | Distinctive | Principled | Carefree | Detailed

The Bohemian archetype is a breath of fresh air. She's a visionary with a heart full of idealism, ethics, and principles. Her lifestyle is a canvas of artistry and unconventionality, where creativity and imaginative ideas flow like a river. She's a dreamer, always looking forward to a brighter future, and she's a fierce advocate for causes she holds dear. Living in the past is not for her; she prefers to dream of what could be.

With her carefree, easy-going demeanour, the Bohemian radiates an aura of peace and calm, drawing people near like a gentle breeze. Folks find her approachable, and conversations flow effortlessly when she's around.

When it comes to style, the Bohemian has an innate sense that's the envy of many. She weaves textures and colours together effortlessly, mixing elements from various eras. Vintage and pre-loved stores are her playground, where she uncovers treasures that others often overlook. Her outfits may seem quirky on anyone else, but look just right on her. Restrictive clothing is a no-go; she revels in the freedom of long, flowing pieces and layers. Earthy, soft colours are her palette, creating unique and imaginative ensembles.

Her love for vintage and pre-loved finds aligns perfectly with her sustainability values, making her wardrobe choices not only fashionable but also eco-friendly. However, in more conventional business-type settings, she might feel a tad uncomfortable. To prepare for such occasions, she can keep a few timeless, structured pieces on standby, ready to blend her Bohemian flair with a touch of professionalism by tapping into the Thinker archetypes.

Pairing her style with elements of the Rock Chick archetype adds a delightful edge, infusing her look with attitude and toughness.

Meet Fiona . . .

Fiona is a family portrait photographer who embodies the Bohemian archetype. Her wardrobe is a delightful mishmash of vintage treasures from charity shops and consignment stores. Fiona's keen eye has a knack for spotting hidden gems, from cowboy boots to hats, all accentuated by her signature beachy waves. Bangles, scarves, crochet, and fringing adorn her accessory collection, reflecting her free-spirited nature.

For Fiona, freedom is paramount, and as she is always drawn to Bohemian-inspired pieces, she needed to get intentional about catering to the Thinker and Do-er areas of her life. When her photography business demands a more serious tone or when formal events arise, she remains true to herself by having a few Sophisticate-inspired outfits ready that are thoughtfully chosen, aligning with the understanding that sometimes, dressing formally is a necessity, even if it doesn't entirely resonate with her true essence. Keeping it simple is the key for her here, so she can still add elements of her Bohemian preferences to her accessories and hair.

On days when tasks demand her focus and productivity, Fiona turns to her collection of Provider-inspired pieces. Comfortable jeans and cosy hoodies help her shift gears and tackle mundane tasks with efficiency. Having the balance in her wardrobe addressed and having outfits prepared for various situations removes the stress from those situations and leaves her free to stay true to her Bohemian soul.

If you are this archetype, great secondary archetypes are . . .

The Sophisticate when you want to be more serious. The Rock Chick or The Athlete when you want to get stuff done.

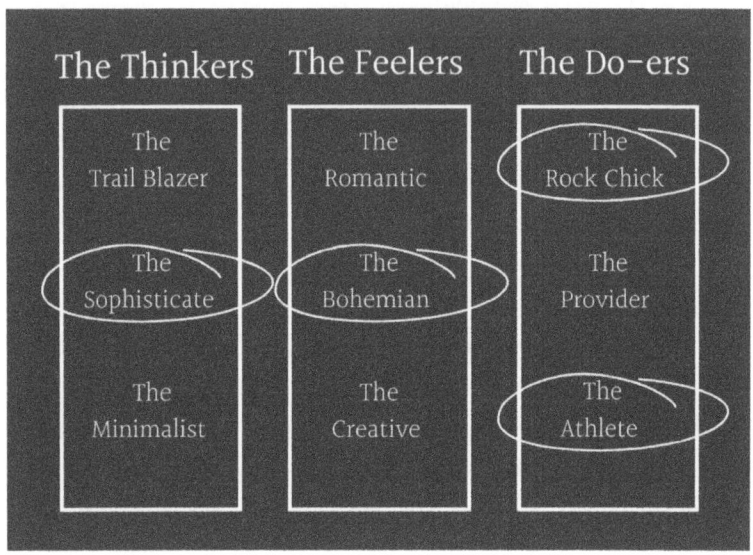

Inspiration for the Bohemian

- ✓ Anything vintage
- ✓ Velvet coats / jackets
- ✓ Embroidered coats / jackets
- ✓ Aviator jackets
- ✓ Long knitted cardigans
- ✓ Waistcoats and vests
- ✓ Denim or fur jackets
- ✓ Romantic maxi dresses
- ✓ Unstructured and oversized tunics, shirts, and blouses
- ✓ Flowing maxi skirts
- ✓ Flared jeans
- ✓ Neutral-coloured ankle boots
- ✓ Tie-dye
- ✓ Suede
- ✓ Prints

✓ Crochet

✓ Lace

✓ Bandanas

✓ Floppy-brimmed hats

✓ Wide-brimmed hats

✓ Scarves that can double up as headbands

✓ Chunky, earthy jewellery

✓ Anything with fringing

✓ Aviator sunglasses

✓ Gladiator sandals

✓ Cowboy boots

✓ Belts

✓ Cross-body bags

✓ Layered jewellery

✓ Crystals and gemstones

THE CREATIVE

Signature Traits

Artistic | Fun | Inventive |Embellished | Colourful

The Creative archetype is all about fun and adventure. She's the embodiment of artistry and unconventionality, and the world recognises her passion for trying new things. Her zest for life inspires those around her to embrace their creative side. When it comes to creative hobbies, she's the go-to guru, showing an affinity for all things handmade and crafted. Conventional dressing is not her cup of tea; she thrives on curating looks that are uniquely her own.

Her wardrobe is a canvas of experimentation, mirroring her love for art and creativity. Colours galore grace her eclectic collection, with rich textures like velvets, embroideries, beading, prints, and all kinds of surface decorations acting as magnetic forces. She champions fellow creatives, seamlessly incorporating their creations into her unique style.

Every day, her wardrobe serves as a wellspring of inspiration, spreading joy wherever she roams. To contain potential creative chaos, the Creative archetype benefits from regular detox sessions and closet curation. Without these, her closet might descend into an artistic abyss.

Like her fellow Feeler archetypes, the Creative should be mindful of including some versatile pieces in her wardrobe for more formal occasions, especially if she aims to be taken seriously in professional settings. Moreover, curating a section of her closet for tackling her to-do list can help her feel in control when life throws unexpected curveballs.

The Creative is a great archetype for all the others to visit when they are looking for inspiration. Taking even tiny elements from this archetype can reinvent and inject a sense of fun into any wardrobe. The Creative archetype is also great to embrace as you age, as the sense of not caring what others think that comes with age is also what feeds the Creative spirit.

Meet Estelle . . .

Estelle is a renowned artist whose closet bursts with colour. Dresses, tunics, flowing skirts, and an array of shirts radiate her artistic spirit. Even on her most understated days, colourful necklaces, bracelets, and earrings complete her outfits, adding that unmistakable touch of creativity.

A challenge many creative people face is the assumption that creatives are not business minded, and while this can be true, Estelle needed to debunk the notion when dealing with people who function in the business world. When Estelle needs to elevate her presence for major projects, client meetings, and gallery showcases, she effortlessly blends her artistic pieces with some structured Trail Blazer items that still resonate with her unique essence. It's all about making a statement that says she's not just an artist but a business-savvy pro too.

We need to acknowledge that creativity *can* sometimes tip the scales toward chaos. On days when she needs a bit more order, Estelle turns to her practical, Provider-inspired pieces. It's like finding her balance in style, keeping her creativity grounded in the midst of daily life.

If you are this archetype, great secondary archetypes are . . .

The Trail Blazer when you want to be more business-like. The Provider when you want to get stuff done.

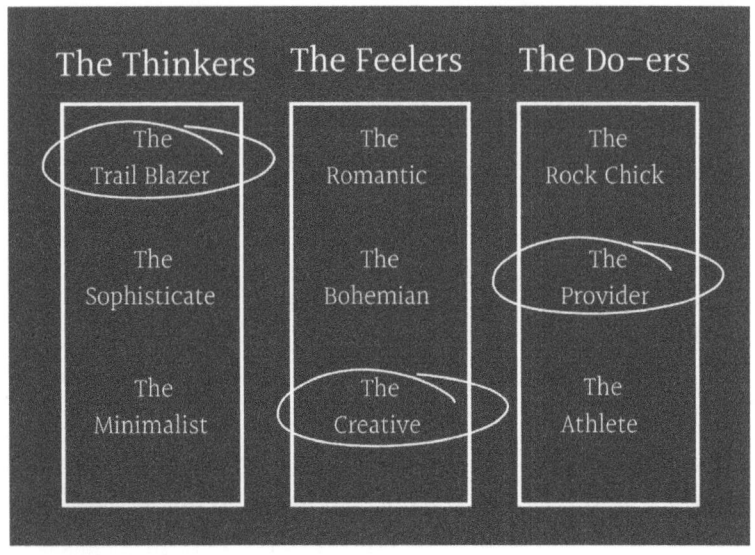

Inspiration for the Creative

- ✓ Anything patchwork
- ✓ Appliqué
- ✓ Colours that mix and match
- ✓ Interesting prints
- ✓ Art on clothes
- ✓ Colourful coats
- ✓ Versatile knitwear
- ✓ Oversized and layered dresses
- ✓ Pinafores and dungarees
- ✓ Maxi dresses
- ✓ Floaty layers
- ✓ Kaftans

- ✓ Handmade jewellery
- ✓ Scarves that can double as headgear
- ✓ Art on / quirky shoes
- ✓ Trainers
- ✓ Coloured and art on hand-bags
- ✓ Handcrafted jewellery
- ✓ Cross-body bags
- ✓ Ceramic and gemstone jew-ellery
- ✓ Sunglasses

CHAPTER 14

THE DO-ER ARCHETYPES

THE PROVIDER
THE ROCK CHICK
THE ATHLETE

"I was dressing for myself and feeling fabulous every day, but I was wondering why I was getting nothing done! I had overlooked the fact that I needed a different version of me for getting through my to-do list."

– RHONA MCMAHON

The Do-ers' Essence: Getting S*** Done

While the Thinkers help you show up as the most power-ful version of you and the Feelers help you show up as the most feminine version of you, the Do-ers archetype group is your go-to when you need to get things done.

This archetype group is all about functionality and action-tak-ing. The Do-ers are your powerhouse for stepping into roles that demand practicality, ease, and dynamic energy. When you want to power through your to-do list and make things happen, the Do-ers are your ultimate allies.

The Do-ers archetype group is your secret weapon for con-quering tasks, so no matter what your role and no matter what level you function at, you will need an element of your wardrobe for practical occasions like getting through a to-do list or even just moving your body.

The Role of the Do-er Archetypes in Your Closet

A lot of busy women, especially mums who are meeting themselves coming back, naturally gravitate towards this archetype group because of its practicality.

If you sit comfortably in this group, you will benefit from intentionally tapping into the other archetype groups for the mindsets that come with them.

The good news is that incorporating other archetypes is easier than it sounds. All it takes is some carefully chosen items on standby in your closet to ensure that you have all your bases covered.

When life requires you to take action and move forward, these Do-er archetypes offer a powerful and efficient approach.

CHAPTER 15

THE ROCK CHICK

Signature Traits

Full of attitude | Edgy | Confident | Spirited | Tough |

The Rock Chick archetype is all about edge and attitude. She exudes confidence and can give off a tough exterior, even though she usually has a soft heart. She's outgoing, with excellent people and communication skills. Always embracing new experiences, she happily shares her newfound knowledge with others.

Friendly, fun, and often the life of the party, she's still considerate of others' feelings.

Her approach to fashion is laid back, favouring jeans, well-worn leather jackets, and biker boots. The more worn her leather jacket looks, the more she adores it. She's drawn to hardware trims and often borrows inspiration and pieces that were designed for men, like jewellery and watches, which perfectly complement her edgy style. She's also a fan of cosy oversized knits, adding a softer dimension to her look.

Her wardrobe is a lifestyle choice that empowers the Rock Chick to take on life without blending into the background. When she wants to infuse some softness into her look, she pairs beautifully with the Romantic archetype, incorporating lace elements and softer fabrics with her leather jackets, knitwear, skinny jeans, and leggings.

Being the Rock Chick offers the freedom to create unique looks, distressing jeans or converting long dresses into shorter, asymmetric-hemmed versions. The more creative and worn, the better. This archetype thrives on mixing unexpected combinations, like pairing flirty dresses with biker boots or satin dresses with leather jackets, experimenting with different fabric textures, from knits to metallics.

Meet Sinead . . .

Sinead is a music producer and the epitome of a Rock Chick. Her wardrobe screams attitude, featuring staples like jeans, biker boots, leather jackets, and oversized jumpers. Her signature look? An effortlessly cool messy bun, whipped up in under thirty seconds flat. Sinead's style sends a bold message: "Don't mess with me." But beneath that edgy exterior lies a softer, more intricate side, and therein lay her biggest challenge. People assumed she was a tough nut, and this was difficult for Sinead emotionally at times. After all, she is just a human.

So, to bring out her softer side, we looked to the Romantic archetype. Looking past how feminine this archetype is, she could see that there were elements of the Romantic that perfectly complimented her staple jeans and tougher outer layers. To bring out her feminine charm, Sinead added soft, lace-trimmed pieces and a subtle touch of soft, feminine colours which seamlessly blend with her Rock Chick aesthetic, achieving that perfect balance and allowing her softer side to shine through.

Sinead has mastered the art of style versatility. When she needs to tap into her sharp business acumen, she's armed with a capsule of Sophisticate-inspired pieces. Picture well-cut dresses with stretch (don't try to restrict her movement) and skirts paired with heels, always with the finishing touch of a leather jacket, preserving her cool, multifaceted persona.

If you are this archetype, great secondary archetypes are . . .

The Sophisticate when you want to be more business-like and *The Romantic* when you want to bring out your feminine side.

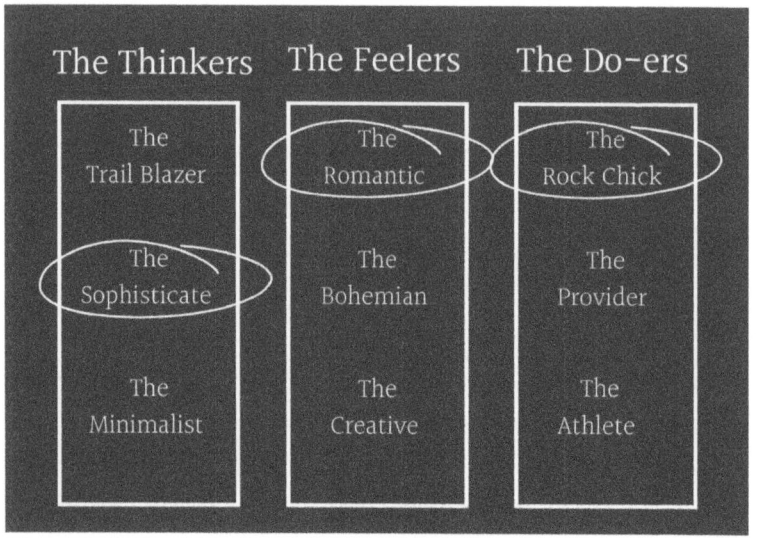

Inspiration for the Rock Chick

- ✓ Leather / denim jacket
- ✓ Boyfriend and chunky hand-knit jumpers
- ✓ Chunky knit cardigans
- ✓ Anything with studs / hardware
- ✓ Faux fur gilets
- ✓ Asymmetrical dresses
- ✓ Vintage dresses
- ✓ Lace / bias-cut skirts
- ✓ Black tulle over pieces / skirts
- ✓ Lace trim camis

- ✓ White shirts
- ✓ White oversized T-shirts
- ✓ Leather skirts
- ✓ Wet-look leggings
- ✓ Skinny jeans
- ✓ Stiletto ankle boots
- ✓ Studded boots
- ✓ Dr Martens
- ✓ White trainers
- ✓ Converse
- ✓ Caps
- ✓ Edgy jewellery

✓ Boyfriend jewellery   ✓ Oversized handbags
✓ Studded belts   ✓ Aviator sunglasses
✓ Chokers

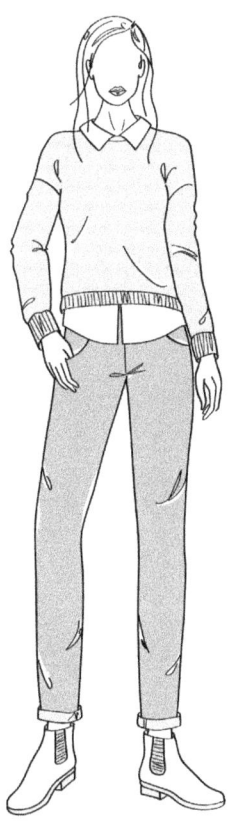

CHAPTER 16

THE PROVIDER

Signature Traits

Comfortable | Practical | Understated | Lifestyle | Casual

The Provider archetype is the one who rolls up her sleeves and gets things done. While others are still contemplating a task, she's often already halfway through it. She's quite comfortable working independently and can move mountains when she's in her element. In times of need, she's the dependable friend who's always willing to lend a hand and make time to help others complete their tasks. You've probably heard the saying "When you want something done, ask the busiest person in the room"–well, that's her. She excels at developing and executing plans and strategies.

Fuss and frills aren't her cup of tea. She prefers practical, everyday clothes that are easy to care for. Her wardrobe is filled with comfortable mix-and-match pieces that effortlessly accommodate her various activities. The Provider is a low-maintenance shopper who values saving time for more important matters.

However, it's essential for the Provider not to slip into the habit of mindlessly reaching for jeans and hoodies every day. Simply throwing on the nearest thing in the morning won't help her step out the door feeling like her best self. Over time, this can impact her self-image and confidence. Using the Provider archetype as an excuse for not caring about her appearance is a slippery slope to invisibility.

The Provider can elevate her wardrobe by borrowing pieces from her sister Do-er archetype, the Rock Chick, which will effortlessly elevate her wardrobe, giving it a welcome injection of attitude. When she wants to bring out her softer self, the Romantic provides inspiration that will fit well into her no-nonsense closet. When she needs to accommodate for formal occasions, a capsule of Sophisticate-inspired outfits will ensure that she is covered for any occasion.

Meet Monika . . .

Monika is a great example of the Provider archetype, working as a dedicated online coach. Her daily wardrobe primarily consists of jeans, tees, hoodies, and skirts–a practical and no-nonsense style that suits her busy life balancing client meetings, household tasks, and school runs. However, like many of us, Monika realised that her lack of intentional dressing had caused her to lose touch with her authentic self. It's an easy trap to fall into when everything else takes precedence.

Together, we embarked on a journey to rediscover Monika's true self and align her goals and how she shows up physically for those. This was the lightbulb moment for her. Her closet was doing nothing to inspire her, so she set about changing that. She started where she was at, removing the things that did not serve her, then assessed what she had left and how she wanted to put it all together. This showed her exactly where the gaps were, and she set the intention of filling those gaps bit by bit with a shopping list that she kept on her phone.

Her wardrobe is still a work in progress, but today, while it still predominantly reflects the Provider archetype, it's now an elevated version of it. This shift allows her to start each day feeling well put together.

When Monika needs to elevate her mindset for strategic thinking or client meetings that demand forward-focused discussions, she has a curated selection of Sophisticate-inspired pieces. These include a great pair of heels and some well-cut simple tops, which empower her to get out the door fast while bringing her A-game to any situation, even on the busiest days.

Monika's non-negotiables in terms of meeting preparation also draw inspiration from the Sophisticate archetype. Polished hair and a simple, pared-back "set" for her Zoom meetings set the right tone, especially for her high-performing clients. Additionally, her closet features well-chosen Romantic-inspired pieces, effortlessly complementing her practical attire and serving as a reminder to slow down and nurture herself when needed.

If you are this archetype, great secondary archetypes are . . .

The Sophisticate when you want to be more business-like, and The Romantic when you want to bring out your feminine side.

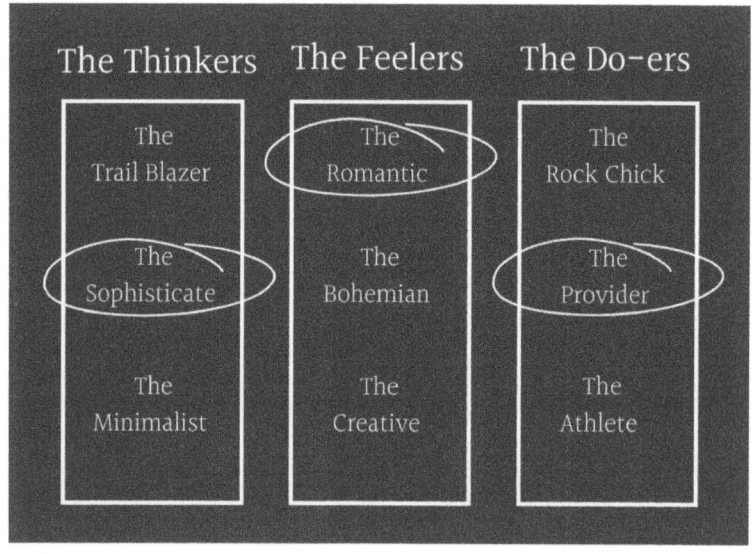

Inspiration for the Provider

✓ *Blazers* ✓ *Bomber jackets*

✓ *Denim jackets* ✓ *Down jackets and vests*

- ✓ Easy-care knitwear
- ✓ Hoodies
- ✓ Cardigans
- ✓ Casual and relaxed dresses
- ✓ Classic shirts and blouses
- ✓ Plaid / white shirts
- ✓ Pinafores and dungarees
- ✓ Jeans
- ✓ Leggings
- ✓ Softly tailored trousers
- ✓ Jersey tops
- ✓ T-shirts
- ✓ Various skirts from straight to A-line, knee length to 3/4 length
- ✓ Trainers
- ✓ Dr Martens
- ✓ Knee-high boots
- ✓ Practical holdall bag
- ✓ Practical cross-body bag
- ✓ Hats and caps
- ✓ Sunglasses

CHAPTER 17

THE ATHLETE

Signature Traits

Sporty | Modern | Understated | Relaxed | Body conscious

The Athlete is the most body-conscious archetype. She is always mindful of her health and fitness and is drawn to sporty and sport-inspired clothes. She is full of energy and always on the go. The other archetypes will often find it hard to keep up with her, and she will still be on the go when the rest have collapsed in a heap.

She needs social interaction and is a great team player. She likes to make life up as she goes along and believes that action is better than perfection.

The Athlete doesn't like to be pinned down and will always choose comfort over style. She loves stretch in everything and feels restricted in structured and fitted non-stretch clothes. The ever-increasing trend towards health and wellness means the athleisure trend she favours is not going anywhere anytime soon. Also, with a significant shift in how people work, and with the gig economy and working from home becoming more popular, this style archetype has slipped into normal everyday workwear.

The Athlete will always want to spend her money on more sporty clothes, so she needs to be intentional and plan for life's other demands on her wardrobe. She may well have to be wrestled away from her gym leggings, so switching them up for a less sporty version and layering them up with relaxed pieces from other style types is a great option for creating a more versatile wardrobe.

The Athlete archetype works particularly well when combined with Rock Chick pieces like knitwear, boots, and biker jackets to add attitude to her wardrobe. Also, there are so many options the Athlete can tap into in the Romantic wardrobe when she wants to bring out her more feminine self. The Minimalist wardrobe also offers shirts, tunics, and knits that she can layer over her Athlete base to ensure that she stays true to herself, even in situations that demand her to show up as if she is not headed to the gym. Elements of the Sophisticate archetype will also suit her very well, especially body-con dresses and separates teamed with a great pair of heels.

Meet Laura . . .

Laura is a physiotherapy PhD student and a true Athlete archetype who radiates an active, sporty aura. Her wardrobe, adorned with sport-inspired clothing, is a testament to her fitness-focused lifestyle. Laura's daily routine is a whirlwind of activity, often leaving others in awe of her boundless energy. She thrives on social interactions and excels as a team player.

Laura's fashion philosophy leans heavily towards comfort, and she cherishes stretchy fabrics that allow her to move freely. Structured and non-stretch clothing feels restrictive to her. Her love for athleisure perfectly aligns with the booming health and wellness trend, making her sporty style versatile enough for everyday wear, including remote workdays.

Laura's challenge was the fact that when she goes shopping, she wants to buy more sporty pieces, but she has this area of her life well covered. The gap in her closet was evident when it came to going out and on special occasions, when she found that putting on makeup and doing her hair just seemed a bit off with everything she had in her closet.

So, she identified the gaps and wrote an intentional shopping list that catered to the other areas of her life. Simply by swapping her colourful gym leggings for a couple of black pairs and adding some black strappy vests, she has created base layers that she can build multiple outfits on, just by layering them with relaxed outer pieces from other archetypes.

The Athlete archetype merges effortlessly with Rock Chick pieces, so Laura used knitwear, biker boots, and a leather jacket to bring our her badass, which she loves. Then she added a touch of Romantic influence, again using her base layers and adding some gorgeous, soft, outer layers and shirt dresses. For occasions that demand a more refined appearance, she tapped into the Sophisticate archetype and completed her closet with body-conscious dresses which show off her physique, completing them with killer heels. These outfits help her feel ready to go for occasions that demand her more serious side to show up.

If you are this archetype, great secondary archetypes are . . .

The Sophisticate when you want to be more business-like. The Romantic when you want to bring out your feminine side.

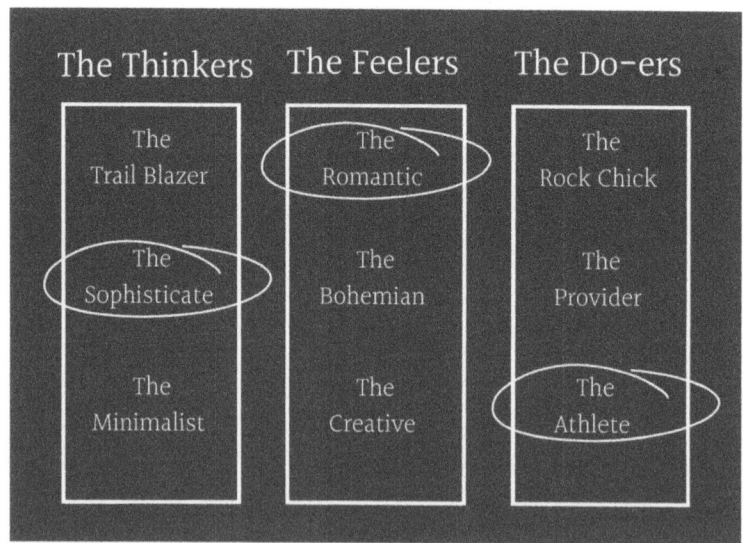

Inspiration for the Athlete

- ✓ Leather / denim jackets
- ✓ Rain / neoprene jackets
- ✓ Oversized / fitted hoodies
- ✓ Oversized knitwear
- ✓ Oversized shirt dresses
- ✓ Skinny jersey dresses
- ✓ Cut-out tops
- ✓ Soft wrap cardigans
- ✓ Soft easy-fit dresses for over leggings
- ✓ Tracksuit bottoms
- ✓ Leggings
- ✓ Cropped hoodies
- ✓ Oversized T-shirts
- ✓ Bralets

- ✓ Cycling shorts
- ✓ High denier tights
- ✓ Gym wear leggings and tops
- ✓ Gym shoes
- ✓ Dance-inspired tops
- ✓ Walking boots
- ✓ Chunky socks
- ✓ Dr Martens
- ✓ Converse
- ✓ Skinny jeans
- ✓ Oversize holdall
- ✓ Caps
- ✓ Chunky scarves
- ✓ Sunglasses

CHAPTER 18

CRAFTING YOUR PERSONAL ARCHETYPE FORMULA

Now that you've explored the archetypes and discovered their unique mindsets, it's time to blend them into a practical formula that resonates with your lifestyle. Think of the archetypes as a toolkit of mindsets, each offering its own set of strengths. In this chapter, we'll discuss how to mix and match these mindsets, build a versatile wardrobe, and adapt your style to different situations.

Blending Archetypes for Your Everyday Style

Just as you wouldn't use only one tool for every task, your style can benefit from combining different archetypes. Maybe you want the confidence of a Thinker for your workdays, but you love the inspiration of the Creative for your weekends. It's all about using the right mindset for the right moment. By blending archetypes, you create a unique style that's both practical and expressive.

Creating a Wardrobe for All Occasions

Your wardrobe is a toolkit for life. You need different tools for different tasks, and similarly, you need different outfits for different occasions.

Different areas of life and various occasions require different versions of you to show up.

Herein lies the power of having your style archetype toolkit to tap into. This toolkit empowers you to effortlessly show up as the best version of yourself in any situation. Crafting your personal archetype formula involves curating a wardrobe that suits your lifestyle. From formal meetings to casual outings and everything in between, your formula ensures you're always dressed with confidence and authenticity. It's about showing up for the day ahead and being prepared for whatever life throws your way.

Adapting to Life's Changes

Life is full of transitions, and your style should be adaptable. Your archetypes can be tailored to fit various situations. When you're stepping into a new role, evolving into a future version of yourself, facing a challenge, celebrating a milestone, or powering through a to-do list, your archetypes can guide you towards showing up powerfully. This adaptability empowers you to confidently embrace every phase of life while staying true to your authentic self.

Your Practical Archetype Toolkit

Crafting your personal archetype formula isn't about creating a complicated system. It's about having a toolkit of mindsets that you can effortlessly switch between. Just as a toolbox helps you tackle different tasks, your archetype toolkit empowers you to handle various situations with confidence and grace. This formula supports you in being true to yourself while navigating life's twists and turns.

As you move forward with your personal archetype formula, remember that this is your practical guide to a more empowered and confident version of you. It's not about following strict rules; it's about using these mindsets as tools to enhance your everyday life. So, embrace your archetypes, mix and match them as needed, and experience the transformation they bring to your style and self-expression.

The coach in me cannot resist giving you an exercise to help you decide what your archetype toolkit will look like.

So here are a few questions to ponder.

* What are your goals and aspirations? What version of you needs to show up for those?

* What are the different mindsets you want to take to the different areas of your life?

UNLEASH YOUR INNER GODDESS

* In terms of the mindsets that go with the archetypes, which do you most resonate with?

The Thinkers	The Feelers	The Do-ers
The Trail Blazer Forward thinking Unique Avant garde	**The Romantic** Soft Feminine Tactile	**The Rock Chick** Spirited Tough Full of attitude
The Sophisticate Polished Chic Glamorous	**The Creative** Artistic Colourful Inventive	**The Provider** Practical Comfortable Casual
The Minimalist Timeless Pared back Quality	**The Bohemian** Vintage Carefree Festival vibes	**The Athlete** Sporty Body conscious Relaxed

* Your **Thinker** archetype is ....

* Your **Feeler** Archetype is ....

* Your **Do-er** archetype is ....

* Which archetype do you have well covered? Which archetype could benefit from a little attention?

Obviously, it's impossible to talk about your wardrobe without delving into body shapes and colour, but before you move on to the next chapter, take a break and ponder what you have discovered about your archetypes. When you are ready, I'll see you there.

EMBRACE YOUR BODY SHAPE

CHAPTER 19

DRESSING YOUR BODY, NURTURING YOUR MIND

Stepping on the weighing scales first thing in the morning is a terrible habit. If you are not happy with where the needle is pointed, it is never going to set you up for a good day. Why would you want to do that to yourself?

Remember, this journey isn't about chasing an unrealistic standard of beauty. It's about embracing your body, celebrating what makes you *you*, and enhancing your style to reflect your inner goddess. As you dive into this chapter, envision a wardrobe that becomes a vehicle of self-expression, a tool that boosts your confidence and nurtures your self-image.

Get ready to uncover the magic of dressing your body and nurturing your mind.

Embracing Your Unique Form

Every woman has aspects of her body she's less than thrilled about–yes, even those who grace magazine covers. In my decades of experience, I've seen models struggle with the same issues as my customers. What's important to remember is that every body is unique, and every body has something to celebrate. We're not here to obsess over perceived imperfections; we're here to amplify our assets.

Highlighting your strengths draws attention away from what you're not as fond of, allowing you to feel confident and empowered in your own skin.

Maybe your captivating eyes deserve centre stage. If that's the case, consider clothing choices that make your eyes pop, helping you forge a direct connection with others.

Perhaps your elegant hands deserve their moment – adorn yourself with sleeves that accentuate their beauty.

If you possess the coveted hourglass figure, let your outfit choices showcase this classic shape.

If your legs go on for days, why not craft outfits that effort-lessly draw the gaze downwards?

The key is to play to your strengths and create a look that represents the best version of you.

Discovering Your Body Shape

In this chapter, we're going to explore the five main body shapes: the Pear, the Apple, the Hourglass, the Column, and the Cornet. By understanding your body shape and learning how to dress it, you're arming yourself with a powerful tool to enhance your personal style.

Imagine the confidence that will radiate from within when you know exactly what outfits flatter your body shape. It's like having a toolkit of fashion wisdom at your fingertips. And here's a secret: you don't have to do it all. Just a few simple tweaks can create an incredible impact, a newfound sense of empowerment that becomes an integral part of your daily life.

Self-love and Acceptance

Remember, this journey isn't about striving for some unreach-able standard; it's about embracing who you are and reflecting this outwardly in how you show up in the world. As we explore each body shape and its ideal clothing choices, keep in mind that these suggestions are here to empower, not confine. Your body shape is unique, and it's a beautiful canvas to express your inner essence.

By understanding how to dress your shape in a way that complements your natural form, you'll be well on your way to confidently curating a wardrobe that perfectly embodies your true self.

How to assess your body type

If you are having trouble identifying which shape you are, take a selfie in your underwear or leggings and a close-fitting tee (preferably black). It is often easier to see shapes in photos than in a mirror. By looking at the body-shape drawings coming up in the next section, you should be able to identify your shape. If you are still not sure, I always find that drawing on a photo makes it more obvious.

CHAPTER 20

THE PEAR

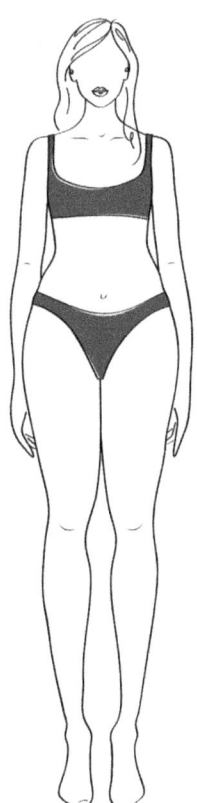

Small bust | Small waist | Hips and thighs are wider than shoulders

This is also known as the triangle shape. If you are a pear, your top half will be narrow and you will have fuller hips and thighs. The goal is always to create a balance. To achieve this, you can add volume to the top part of your body while wearing slimmer pieces on the bottom.

Looking Great as a Pear

You probably have a well-defined shape and a great waist, so show it off! Use padded bras to give you extra fullness at the bust area. Boat necks, off-the-shoulders, and wide scoop necklines will show off your defined and slim shoulders. Prints on the top half of your body, matched with a plain darker colour on the bottom, can also create balance, with the dark colour visually reducing your hip size. Billowing tops nipped in at the waist will look fab on you and create fullness on your top half.

What to Wear

✓ Frills and flounces on sleeves

✓ Embellishments at the shoulders and neckline

✓ Light fullness in skirts and dresses

✓ Wide-leg pants in darker colours

✓ Wrap shirts and tops with a fitted waist

✓ A-line skirts

✓ Strapless dresses with full skirts

✓ Cinched waist jackets with shoulder and sleeve details

✓ Structured coats with belt details at the waist

✓ Jeans with fading on the thigh area

What to Avoid

✓ Cigarette pants

✓ Balloon dresses

✓ Mini skirts

✓ Bright colours on the lower half

✓ Bias-cut skirts

CHAPTER 21

THE APPLE

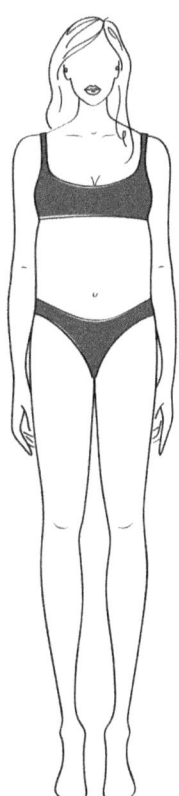

Big bust | Undefined waist | Small hips | Slim arms | Slim legs

You may find that when you put on a bit of weight, it lands on your tummy area. Do not let it get into your headspace and drive you crazy. You can draw attention away from this and focus on your best assets. These are often your lovely slim legs and arms, so you want to highlight those by wearing fitted items there.

Looking Great as an Apple

The first job is to get fitted for a good supportive bra, which will stop the girls from wandering. Use vertical lines to draw the eye down your body. This can be done with long necklaces and scarves, as well as vertical seams and details. Short, chunky necklaces will also draw attention up to your face. Avoid horizontal lines, which will chop you in two.

One of my favourite ways to dress this body shape is to use ruching diagonally across the body, which draws the eye down. The ruching also creates wrinkles, which visually reduce the size of any area where they appear.

What to Wear

✓ V-neck / scoop-neck tops

✓ Shirts and T-shirts ruched in the middle

✓ Soft, textured fabrics

✓ A-line skirts and dresses

✓ Soft, flared trousers

✓ Dresses that flow from under the bustline

✓ Tops that fall lower than the hip bone

✓ Jackets with well-defined shoulders

✓ Flat-front trousers

✓ Ruched and draped tops with open necklines

✓ Tops that flare from under the bustline

✓ Straight-front jackets and cardis (long, straight lines that draw the eye down the body)

✓ Straight duster coats

✓ Any lines that draw the eye downwards

What to avoid

- ✓ Anything too fitted
- ✓ Coarse textures
- ✓ Shapeless, boxy items

- ✓ Details near the waist
- ✓ Turtlenecks
- ✓ Horizontal stripes

CHAPTER 22

THE HOURGLASS

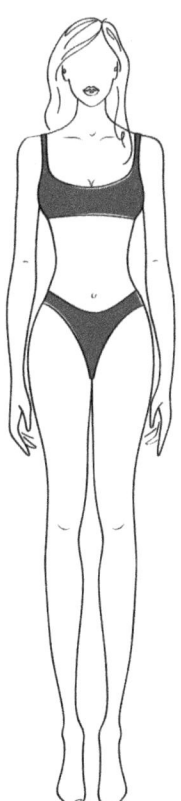

Generous bust | Small waist | Generous hips and thighs

This is the most classically feminine body type; you are a goddess! This is also seen as the sexiest body type. If you have it, lucky you–embrace it! Your bust and hip lines are well balanced. Your waist is defined and you are in proportion.

Looking Great as an Hourglass

The key to dressing this most feminine body type is to keep the top and bottom of your body in proportion while accentuating your waist. Simple lines with a well-defined waist will look great on you. Adding belts to flowing and simple tops will allow you to add light volume and femininity without losing your shape. The trick to wearing anything floaty and romantic is to keep it transparent and wear something fitted underneath so that you can still clearly see the outline of your body.

What to Wear

- ✓ A well-fitted, supportive bra
- ✓ Simple lines with a well-defined waist
- ✓ Wrap, fitted, or belted tops and dresses
- ✓ Add a belt to simply cut flowing tops

- ✓ Tailored shirts and jackets that nip in at the waist
- ✓ Deep V and scoop necklines
- ✓ Draped, flowing pants
- ✓ Open necklines
- ✓ Slim body-con skirts

What to Avoid

- ✓ Frilly shirts
- ✓ Big bows
- ✓ Lots of volume

- ✓ Chunky knits
- ✓ High necklines
- ✓ Baggy clothes

CHAPTER 23

THE CORNET

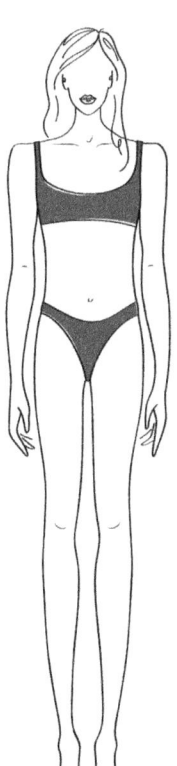

Broad shoulders | Small bust | Undefined waist | Slim hips | Long legs

You have strong shoulders and a slim body. You are the perfect clothes hanger, and while you may sometimes long for curves, you have the body of a supermodel. You can wear anything and look fabulous! For you, the art is about creating curves where they may seem absent and knowing the very few things you should try to avoid.

Looking Great as a Cornet

Asymmetrical lines in soft, floaty fabrics will look ethereal and fabulous on you, as will any cuts which create curves around the body. Soft ruching and diagonal tucks and folds can be belted in interesting ways. Patterns that vary in size and shape will also create the impression of curves. Slashed and asymmetrical necklines will look great on you, reducing the width of your shoulders and creating balance with your slim hips.

What to Wear

- ✓ Long or short sleeves
- ✓ Wide shoulder straps
- ✓ Ruffles on your upper body
- ✓ Draping and gathers
- ✓ Anything that exaggerates your hips

- ✓ Fitted shoulders
- ✓ A-line dresses and skirts
- ✓ Long dresses
- ✓ Angled pockets
- ✓ Asymmetrical panelling

What to Avoid

- ✓ ¾ length sleeves
- ✓ Baggy, shapeless dresses
- ✓ Spaghetti straps

- ✓ Deeply scooped necklines
- ✓ Masculine cuts when you want to feel more feminine

THE COLUMN

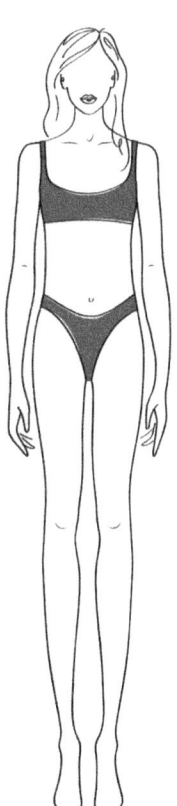

Shoulder and hip width the same | Slight waist | Long legs

This body shape is often described as the racehorse of the group. You have long limbs, are statuesque, and may be quite tall. You may have been teased for having a body like a boy as a teenager. That was stressful then, but you can really rock this body shape now as you can wear almost anything!

Looking Great as a Column

The Column-shaped body does have curves, but these are stretched out over your length. You can use volume to create curves anywhere you want them, so there are many opportunities for you to play around with different looks and very few restrictions. The main thing to be conscious of is that wearing long, fitted lines will make you appear taller.

What to Wear

- ✓ Different blocks of colour on the top and bottom to break up your long frame
- ✓ Flared trousers
- ✓ A-line skirts
- ✓ Single-button jackets
- ✓ Bias-cut dresses
- ✓ ¾ length belted coats
- ✓ Cropped trousers
- ✓ Round-necked jumpers
- ✓ Gathered shirts
- ✓ Belted tube tops
- ✓ Wide belts in darker colours
- ✓ Boat necks
- ✓ Off-the-shoulder tops
- ✓ Flowing and billowing tops, belted
- ✓ Embellishments at bust and shoulders
- ✓ Structured-shoulder jackets

What to Avoid

- ✓ Straight dresses in one colour
- ✓ Boxy jackets
- ✓ Cropped tops
- ✓ Dropped waists

CHAPTER 25

A NOTE ON HEIGHT

Height is something that crops up time and time again, no matter what body shape people have. I come across so many women who just want to be a few inches taller but don't want to wear heels.

There's a huge choice on the market of platform or wedge shoes that will give you the height you desire while still allowing you to run around.

A favourite tip though, especially for people with short legs, is to wear nude heels that match your skin tone, which add several inches to the length of your legs!

THE POWER
OF COLOUR

CHAPTER 26

CHOOSE YOUR COLOUR PALETTE

As with everything in this book, choosing a specific colour palette is not about limiting your options; it's about creating a harmonious wardrobe ecosystem. By selecting colours that resonate with you and work seamlessly together, you're setting the stage for endless mix-and-match possibilities. This approach makes accessorising effortless and ensures that each piece in your closet contributes to expanding your outfit options.

Imagine starting your day knowing that as long as you have clean clothes hanging in your closet, you will have effortless outfit options. A well-curated colour palette offers you convenience and the assurance that your outfits will consistently be a powerful outward reflection of your inner world.

Embrace Your Colour Story

As we explore the realm of colours, consider the emotions you want to evoke and the impressions you wish to leave. Discover how different shades resonate with your personality and boost your confidence. This chapter isn't just about picking attractive colours; it's about crafting your own colour story–a narrative of empowerment, self-expression, and authenticity.

Curating Your Colour Palette

It is quite likely that you will favour one particular group of colours in your wardrobe. If you stick to this one group, you will find that your individual garments work better together.

A simple way to get visual insights is to open your closet and remove anything that you don't wear. What remains tells a story about your colour preferences. Let these be the foundation for building your wardrobe and your guide for future choices.

The more tightly you curate your closet, the more powerfully it will support you. As you throw open the doors each morning, you will be greeted by choices that speak to the mindset work you have previously invested in, so you can just grab something from the hanger and go. This is the key to showing up effortlessly. I keep repeating "effortlessly" because that is the win I am gifting to you when you invest in doing this work for yourself.

Once you have curated your colour palette, be protective of it. Don't let weak moments or random purchases into your closet. Believe me, I know how easily this can happen. It took me about three years of doing this work to realise that the random purchases end up sitting on the rail gathering dust. They hijack your spending power when it comes to investing in the things you really want.

The biggest takeaway I want you to get from this is . . .

Be the gatekeeper.

Nothing gets into your closet that doesn't work with what you already have!

Neutrals

Black | White | Grey | Brown | Naturals | Metallics

Neutrals go with everything and mix and match effortlessly with each other. These are essential for building every woman's wardrobe.

Choosing a whole wardrobe of neutrals may seem boring. However, doing so speaks of a woman's confidence, especially when iconic statement pieces mix and match, forming the building blocks of a timeless wardrobe.

My favourite way to introduce interest into a neutral wardrobe is in textures. Think of metallics, hardware, knits, soft and silky fabrics, leather, shiny mixed with matte . . . The options are endless. You can keep it simple, or mix several of these together to create a look that goes from Minimalist on one end of the scale to Trail Blazer on the other.

The key to the success of the neutrals wardrobe is to rejuvenate it each season, moving the look along to stay relevant. This can be done over time–adding just one or two investment pieces each season can both reinvent everything you have in your closet and remind you that "you are worth it" when you wear them.

Soft and earthy colours

Pastels | Whites | Stones and sands | Blue | Green | The colours of nature

You can build a whole wardrobe around soft and earthy colours. It will require more ongoing thinking than a neutral palette, as you will need to be intentional about how you mix your colours unless you choose single-item outfits.

Of course, opinions on colour vary greatly, and you will no doubt find plenty of people who will disagree with me on this, but these are my insights from over thirty years of curating my fashion collections and co-ordinating looks for photoshoots.

Broadly speaking, there are two subgroups in the soft and earthy group. You have the pastels, and the autumnal and berry colours. Most people I have worked with will generally have a preference for one group over the other. If you find you are drawn to both, I suggest keeping them separated to make it easier to create outfits, as you will probably use them in different ways. For example, you may go for a softer palette in Summer and a stronger palette in Winter.

The pastels work beautifully together for soft, feminine looks. You can mix and match them–the key to success here is choosing similar tones. My favourite tip for doing this is when you see images of nature that appeal to you, drag them into a colour picker app and it will show you all the individual colours. Another tip that I use all the time involves looking at paint sample charts. They are a great way to see how different colours work together.

The stronger autumnal and berry colours are great for single item outfits. They will require more work if you want to mix the colours. This is not a problem if you are happy to spend the time doing this, but if not, it might feel like hard work to you. A great way to see what colours work together is to look at colours opposite each other on a colour wheel. Opposites work together.

Vibrant colours

Red | Yellow | Orange | Strong blues, greens, pinks | Neon

The vibrant colours are the fun colours of the family. If you like to stand out and be memorable, this may be the colour palette you gravitate towards. For this reason, the vibrant colour palette is great if you want to have dresses on standby for occasions like corporate events, presentations, speaking, awards, business meetings, and so on . . .

It is important to be aware that outfits that make a bold statement are also less versatile, and you may not get as much wear out of them as you might with similar investments in the neutral colour palette. If budget is not an issue, great, but it is a consideration otherwise.

The vibrant colour palette works great for individual pieces, but it is also amazing for mixing colours and creating loud, bold statements. The Creative archetype will live in this colour palette, creating outfits that only she can pull off. It is also a good option for a Trail Blazer who likes colour and a Sophisticate who likes dresses.

If you prefer not to have vibrant colours as your wardrobe building blocks but would still like a bit of this colour palette, consider using vibrant colours in shoes, accessories, bags, and glasses or even just a red lip.

A Note on Colours and Workwear

It is worth mentioning some colour tips for work situations. When you want to just get on with things, fly under the radar, and fade into the background, wear low-contrast outfits. Colour combinations like browns, beiges, and greens suggest that you would like to be left alone. They give off a low-energy, forgettable vibe, but it's useful to know this for those days when you just want to get through that long to-do list!

You might not give off the vibe of setting the world on fire if you wear medium-contrast outfits, such as a black skirt and a pale blouse, but you will be seen as dependable and reliable. This combination is always a safe bet for work if you are unsure what is appropriate.

Wearing high-contrast outfits, like a dark skirt, a light top, and a pop of colour in a scarf or accessories, speaks of confidence and being comfortable in positions of responsibility. It is the pop of brightness that does this. (Think of airline uniforms, which often have a pop of red in their colour scheme.)

CHAPTER 27

UNLOCK THE PSYCHOLOGY OF COLOUR

Colours hold the power to influence your mood, emotions, and even how others perceive you. Understanding the psychology of colour empowers you to make choices that align with your intentions. The colours you wear play an important role in helping you to show up with the most empowered version of you in any situation. The colours you choose can boost any emotion, from passion to contentment to serenity. They have the potential to help you stand out, create an inviting aura, or even diffuse confrontational situations.

So, let's dive into the captivating world of colours. By understanding their psychology and curating a personalised palette, you're opening the door to a wardrobe filled with limitless possibilities.

Bear in mind that the influence of colour on emotions can also depend on personal and cultural associations. Different people may have varying emotional responses to the same colours based on their experiences and backgrounds.

Black

Sophisticated | Serious | Intelligent | Powerful | Dark

People who wear black are seen as being serious and diligent. They are also often sensitive and emotional, although they can come across as being quite tough and will not always admit it. If you wear black a lot, well-meaning family and friends may well tell you not to buy more black. We heard it so often over the years on the shop floor. And what did these people end up buying? Yes, more black! It is by far the most popular colour in fashion–sorry, guys! Black will always be the new black!

Tips for wearing black

- Wear it when you want to impress! Have a little black dress, even if it's the only piece of black in your wardrobe. It will see you dressed for any formal occasion.
- Add pops of colour to soften black and add interest.
- Be aware that as we get older, our complexion changes and all-black can look quite harsh. So, keep an eye on it and soften it as you get older, especially if you favour dying your hair black.

- Be careful of black if you tend to have dark shadows under your eyes, as black close to your face can accentuate them.

- Wear black tourmaline gemstones to keep you grounded and to clear negativity.

White

Meticulous | Free | Pure

White is the colour of cleanliness, innocence, and purity. Wearing it implies that you are an organised and detail-oriented person. Some old rules about wearing white suggest that it can only be worn in the summer. It can be worn all year round, just be selective in the pieces that you wear. For example, a white shirt is always going to work, and winter white always looks great, even on the most wintery days.

Tips for wearing white

- Wear it colour blocked with black for dramatic, powerful outfits.

- If you find it can wash you out, break it up with other colours.

- Be aware that plain undergarments that match your skin tone are a good choice, whereas patterns and lace may well show through white clothing.

- Everyone can wear white; you just need to find the right one for your skin tone.

- Apply your perfume before getting dressed and your makeup after getting dressed to avoid staining.
- Wear white selenite gemstones to release stuck energy and achieve balance.

Grey

Balanced | Tranquil | Dimensional

Grey is one of those neutral colours that, on its own, does not define somebody's personality. However, if you wear a lot of grey, you may fade into the background. It can be seen as the colour of maturity or of somebody flying under the radar. It does work well in a wardrobe of neutral colours and blacks. It also looks incredible on people with grey hair, especially when worn with soft pinks and lavenders.

Tips for wearing grey

- Wear it with darker or more intense colours.
- Wear it with a pop of colour in your accessories.
- Wear it with soft pinks and neutral peachy colours for a sophisticated look.
- Be careful of wearing pale greys from head to toe; it could end up looking washed out.
- Colour block with black for a sophisticated but softer look than head-to-toe black.
- Wear grey moonstone gemstones to enhance intuition and patience and get in touch with your more feminine side.

Brown

Earthiness | Reliability| Strength | Dullness

Brown is the colour of the earth, so people who wear it are seen as being earthy, calm, and grounded. They are often seen as rational and intelligent, conservative and respectful of other people. People who favour brown tend to seek peace and stability.

Tips for wearing brown

- Wear it in situations when you want to be seen as strong, reliable, and trustworthy.
- Mix it with colours like orange and yellow for harmony.
- Brown and beige are a natural pairing that never goes out of style.
- Mixed with white, brown is very chic.
- Don't use too much of the same tone; mix it with some black details to spice it up.
- Wear brown tiger's eye gemstones to reduce overwhelm, become non-reactive in stressful situations, and stay centred.

Blue

Kind | Trustworthy | Calm | Trusting | Sad

Navy is a great softer alternative to black, especially in the summer. Blue is known to slow down human metabolism and have a calming effect on the psyche. Often if you ask people what their favourite colour is, they will say blue. It is the colour of the sky, the colour of the sea; it is everywhere in nature and is associated with peace and tranquillity. It has a peaceful effect on people around you. This is also the reason that many people use it in bedrooms.

Tips for wearing blue

- Wear for interviews, as it conveys confidence and reliability.
- Wear navy with bright whites for a sharp and chic look.
- Wear darker shades of blue when you want to have a calming effect.
- Wear navy and pale blues for business to inspire confidence.
- Wear it when you are feeling stressed, as it has a calming effect.
- Wear blue larimar gemstones when you want to promote peace, confidence, and clear communication.

Green

Growth | Harmony | Envy

The colour of nature, green, is calming and easy on the eye. It can also be seen as the colour of envy and greed, so be careful not to wear too much of it. It is not the colour to wear if you want to set the world on fire, but on the other hand, green is also seen as the colour of luck, so wear it if you are feeling a little bit superstitious. Green can also mean you are full of life, healthy, and environmentally aware. It is the colour used for many eco-friendly products and is also the colour of healing.

Tips for wearing green

- Don't wear head-to-toe green in a work situation if you are looking for a promotion; you will fade into the background.

- Wear it with florals for a fresh springtime look.

- Added as a pop of colour to black, it can be a great accent colour for work.

- Wear green when you want to feel grounded and connected to nature.

- Wear green serpentine gemstones to support you in transition and being true to yourself.

Red

Passion | Anger | Love | Energy

Red is the colour of energy and passion. When you wear red, you will most certainly be noticed. While red is perceived as being a sexual colour, studies have shown that a subtle pop of red is more suggestive than an all-out red outfit. You can also use pops of red around your house in areas where you want to boost the energy.

Tips for wearing red

- Wear red from top to toe if you want to stand out.

- Wear with black or white for business.
- Choose a red that works with your skin tone. (Ask for help with this at your favourite makeup counter.)
- Wear a red dress for a classic, feminine look.
- Wear a pop of red in accessories or lippy if all-out red feels too much for you.
- Wear red ruby gemstones when you want to overcome fears and obstacles and accomplish big goals.

Yellow

Happiness | Adventure | Optimism | Caution

Yellow increases the production of serotonin in the brain and improves the mood of everyone around you when you wear it. People who wear yellow are seen as happy, optimistic, and adventurous. They are often creative people who are ready to explore and conquer the next opportunity. Yellow flowers on your desk or around your house are great for getting inspired.

Tips for wearing yellow

- Wear it when you or people around you need cheering up.
- Wear yellow stripes if solid yellow is too much for you.
- Wear it solid on the bottom with more subtle prints on top.
- Wear it as an accent colour in accessories.
- Wear it in winter to add a bit of sunshine to dark days.

- Wear yellow sapphire gemstones to turbocharge your vitality and sustain your vision when your energy is low.

Purple

Creative | Insightful | Sophisticated | Mysterious

Purple is rare in nature and expensive to create, which means that throughout history it has been associated with royalty and the privileged in society. It is also associated with supernatural powers (good to know, yes?). Light purples are light-hearted and romantic, while darker shades are more intellectual. Wearing purple helps to boost creativity and imagination, but too much of it can create moodiness. It is very useful when calming confrontational situations, and it also helps to create energy around learning new things.

Tips for wearing purple

- Purple makes every eye colour pop, so wear it close to your face when you want to connect with people.

- Wear it as a pop of colour with black or grey if you are not sure about wearing a full outfit in it.

- Some would say you shouldn't mix purple with other colours, but red and purple make a dramatic combination that works well in colour blocking. Consider purple as an accent colour with neutrals like taupes, silvers, metallic whites, bronzes, and pewters.

- Lavender, paler shades of purple, and light lavender-greys are amazing with blonde or grey hair.

- Wear purple rhodonite gemstones when you want to get clarity on your goals and unique gifts.

Pink

Love | Playfulness | Sweetness | Calm

Traditionally, pink has been seen as girly, flirty, and uber-feminine. For this reason, it is often shunned by people who want to be taken seriously. However, pale pinks are calm, warm, and non-aggressive, so some soft pinks are a great addition to a working wardrobe when you want to show up as the softer version of yourself. At the other end of the pink scale is hot pink, which is a great girl-boss colour and when worn with black, can be quite edgy. Pink represents affection, friendship, approachability, and harmony.

Tips for wearing pink

- Wear pink to promote happiness in those around you.
- Wear hot pink to communicate playfulness.
- Wear light pink to communicate tenderness.
- Pale pink is a great colour to wear when you want to wind down at night, or to sleep in. Cosy pale-pink blankets will have the same effect on everybody in your household.
- Wear pink gemstones for serenity, relaxation, contentment, and to soften frustration.

Orange

Energy | Warmth | Enthusiasm | Fun

Orange is a playful colour that promotes learning and energy. It is a mix of red and yellow, so it is also a mixture of those colour personalities. Use orange if you want to feel young and carefree. It can be bright and overpowering, so use it in moderation, especially in tense situations.

Tips for wearing orange

- Add it as an accent colour to neutrals across the spectrum, from blacks to beiges and whites.

- If you are feeling brave, wear it with purple. If bright orange feels like too much, consider more peachy tones or add some playful orange accessories for summer.

- Give orange a try; the right tone for your skin will make it glow.

- Be careful of wearing with black–you don't want to look like Halloween!

CURATE
YOUR
PERSONAL
STYLE

CHAPTER 28

SEVEN MISTAKES THAT CRIPPLE YOUR STYLE

"Your closet can either inspire or frustrate you.
The choice is yours."

— MARY GRANT

In the hustle and bustle of life, our closets often bear witness to our ever-evolving stories. Over time, without conscious intention, our closets can transform into a chaotic maze of random purchases, clothes that no longer fit, and pieces from eras long gone.

We open the doors to our closet each day, hoping for inspiration yet are frequently greeted with frustration. But here's the captivating truth: your closet holds immense power. It is not just a collection of garments; it's an anthology of possibilities waiting to empower you.

The question is, will you let your closet be the source of inspiration and the catalyst for unleashing your inner goddess, or will you let it hold you back?

Over three decades of observation and conversations with my customers, these are the seven most common mistakes we all make that result in a closet full of pieces that do nothing to serve us.

Why We Need to Call Out These Mistakes

I know, I know, nobody likes to hear about the mistakes they make. But it's important that you start to notice mistakes that may be holding you back, in order to break the cycle and prevent yourself from getting stuck in a rut. So, let's just fly through them really quickly. You may recognise some or all of them. Any combination of them can result in a bulging wardrobe of clothes that do not serve you.

These habits are quick fixes that scratch an itch for five minutes, but they do nothing to make you feel joyful or inspired in the long run. Understand them and you will be one step closer to building a wardrobe that works for you long term. And, as a result, you will only spend your money on things that bring you joy and serve you well over time.

Don't let the mistakes of the past invade your headspace. We often beat ourselves up or waste time justifying things that haven't served us well. Seriously, nobody cares, move on. Forget the mistakes, hold on to the lessons.

Mistake #1
Following trends

Trends are not gospel. They are merely a reflection of what is happening in the world at that moment. Don't allow them to dictate what you buy. It's good to know what is on-trend, as you can use this information to make sure you are relevant. However, you should curate those trends so that they suit your lifestyle, personality, and body shape. If you do the work, your confidence in choosing the pieces that are right for you will already have grown by the time you get to the end of this book, and you will continue to grow as you practise what you learn in the coming chapters. Although you will still value the input of experts who can suggest what might work for you, you won't need anybody else to tell you what to wear.

Mistake #2
Buying clothes that don't work with what you already have

It's a magpie moment. You spot that bright, new shiny thing. You feel an emotional attraction to it, but once you get it home, you wonder what on earth you were thinking. It doesn't work with anything you have already, and it just sits there in your wardrobe, like a Billy-no-mates. You keep promising yourself that you will wear it, but either it never happens, or you only wear it rarely because you don't have a variety of ways to wear it.

Mistake #3
Not buying the things you love

Getting over this is one of the best-kept secrets for building a wardrobe that serves you for many years. You cannot truly appreciate it until you break out and do it once. Only then will you see what I mean. How many times have you lusted after a piece that was just "so you" but didn't buy it, either because you thought it was too expensive or you thought about it so much that you talked yourself out of it? You know, that one piece you were still thinking about days later? It was a timeless piece you would wear time and time again over its lifetime, but what did you do instead? You opted for a few cheaper, average alternatives, and the money was spent anyway. As a result, you either did not wear those pieces or ended up giving them away a few months later. The next time you find something that you love, think about all the times you will wear it and what the cost per wear will be. Something that you wear regularly over years will owe you nothing in the long run.

Mistake #4
Waiting for the sales

There are a few problems with this, and they will all leave you feeling disappointed and unfulfilled. We all love to bag a bargain, but it has to be the right bargain, and if you only shop in this way, your conscious mind is telling your subconscious that you only deserve the cheap stuff.

When you wait for the sales, you will probably miss out on the one piece you really want, or your size will be nabbed by the person who walked in the door just before you. Our team saw this all the time in our stores. The other problem with this approach is that you acquire pieces at the end of a season and have little opportunity to wear them until the following year. You would do better to buy your pieces at the start of the season so you can enjoy wearing them, feeling both fabulous and empowered by them all season long. You will reap the rewards many times over.

Mistake #5
Last-minute shopping

This is when a lot of mistakes are made. A last-minute invite or an event has snuck up on you. Suddenly, you are under pressure to get something to wear. This is never a good shopping experience. You will feel the stress of the deadline and rarely enjoy it. You will often end up buying things that you are not in love with. They will do fine for the event, but they rarely see the light of day afterwards.

You will never find things you love when you are shopping under pressure. You will find things that you love when you are relaxed and not looking for anything in particular.

You will usually find more things that you love when you are already feeling inspired and empowered. The right mindset makes all the difference, and as with so many things, like attracts like. When you are already dressed up and feeling great, you are much more likely to find something else that you love.

Mistake #6
Buying clothes that do not suit your body shape

I've worked with models for thirty years, and I can tell you that every single woman I have ever met (including the models!) has some body issue, something that she doesn't like. We get way too hung up on these things. Too often, people shop for the shape and size that they think they will be in six months. This is never a good idea. You will only be empowered today by dealing with what you have today. Just get clear on your shape and play down the bits that you do not want to draw attention to.

Mistake #7
Spending too much on outfits for occasions

If there is one thing I could change as a designer who wants to see women being the most confident versions of themselves every day, it is this. Special occasions prompt shopping trips, and people end up spending a fortune on things that they only wear once or twice. The rest of the time, they look in their wardrobes and think, "I have nothing to wear." Your clothing budget should be spent according to how often you will wear the pieces you buy. Everyday pieces that make you step out of your front door every day ready to take on the world are worth investing in. When it comes to occasions, consider choosing simpler pieces you can keep changing up by varying your hairstyle and accessories.

The Way Forward

I promise you, if you ditch these buying mistakes it will change your life! You will see the following benefits:

Spend less money

Now, I'm not telling you you shouldn't be spending money. It's not about that. It's about eliminating impulse buys. When you curate your closet, you will always have options, no matter what occasion arises. So, events, invitations, and special occasions will no longer prompt buying trips. Over time, this will save you a fortune that you can put to better use. You can also repurpose saved funds towards pieces that you really want that will serve you over many years.

Create more time

Again, special and one-off occasions won't prompt buying trips. Over the years, I have seen customers fall in our door after hours of traipsing around shops looking for outfits for special occasions. That's whole Saturdays that you will find right there . . . time you can invest in the things you actually *want* to be doing!

Be inspired every morning

When I hit forty and got stuck in a rut, I hated everything in my closet. It was a huge job to curate it, so you can expect it to be a big job for you, too, the first time you tackle it. When I was finished, I promised myself I would never have to do that kind of heavy lifting again.

When you have a closet that you have spent time curating, you won't *want* to let random stuff in there. You will become the gatekeeper. This is a life-changing mindset shift that radiates into every single area of life.

Let nothing into your closet that hasn't earned its place.

CHAPTER 29

THE NINE LIES WE TELL OURSELVES

Lies and Limiting Beliefs

A number of lies or unconscious biases can lurk beneath the surface where you may not even be aware of them. My team saw them all the time on the shop floor. Our customers are often totally unaware of them until we bring them to their attention. Once you become aware of them and see how they are holding you back, you can choose to tell yourself a different story and open up all kinds of new possibilities.

Which ones do you recognise?

Lie #1
I'm too old . . .

Says who? You can be young until the day you die, and you don't need anybody else's approval or permission for this. If you think about it, no matter what age our body says we are, we can feel exactly the same on the inside in our forties and fifties as we did in our twenties and thirties.

You only start to feel old if you let society's expectations and biases influence you. There is nothing like laughter, learning, and silliness to keep you young. I'm not suggesting that you dress like a twenty-year-old when you are in your forties or fifties—anything but! But nurture a sense of adventure and let it shine through in how you present yourself to the world.

Lie #2
I'm too short . . .

I would just like to reframe that for you. I've always thought that I'm too tall, so you really can't win. We have to be happy with what we've been dealt in life and work with what we've got.

You can add height with heels or platform soles. I know women who are five foot nothing and you would never know it because they are intentional about their footwear.

If you are inspired by an outfit on somebody taller than you and find yourself thinking it would never work for you, a quick reframe is asking yourself, "What version of that would work for me?"

Lie #3
I'll be happy / more confident when I'm thinner / more successful . . .

I have seen far too many women settling for clothes that do not empower them because they are waiting to be thinner to feel more confident. This is backwards. If you find yourself thinking this, get rid of anything that doesn't fit you. Put it out of your sight. It is not inspiring you winking at you from the rails when you cannot fit into it.

Start with a handful of pieces that all work for you right now. Here is the mindset shift: when you already feel good, you are more likely to do more of the right things to move in the direction you want to go.

Focus on your assets and highlight those. Practise complimenting yourself on your assets, your efforts, and being happy with where you are at today, and you will attract more of it tomorrow.

Lie #4
I need to be going somewhere to justify buying that . . .

I am going to repeat this because sometimes repetition is a gift. Special occasions prompt buying trips. This is a fact that we saw time and time again in our stores. People would save up for a wedding outfit, often spending €600–€700 or more on an outfit for one day. The thing about that was–and I saw this time and time again–people would deny themselves the things that would empower them every day in order to buy something that they would only wear for one day.

So, I would love for you to think about all the times you have done this. Maybe you buy the cheapest jeans you can find and think you need several different types. You don't. Find the best pair for you in a range that specialises in jeans, and when you find the perfect fit, buy two or three pairs exactly the same. You will be amazed how this makes you feel when you wear them and how it impacts how you feel about your wardrobe. Think about something else you may have denied yourself over the years . . . Maybe it was a great leather jacket or a winter coat, but you went with a cheaper option. Those are pieces that will serve you for many years. You can just pull them out year after year, and they will elevate all your wardrobe options.

Invest in the pieces that make you feel great and wear them *all the time!*

Lie #5
I'm not the kind of person who could wear that . . .

This thinking can really hold you back from evolving.

A great example of this is to think about a time you admired something that somebody was wearing. In our stores, people would admire what our stylists were wearing and then add, "but I could never do that." The only difference is, the stylist did it every day. It had become second nature.

When you find yourself having this thought, assess what has caught your eye through the filter of whether it can be worked into your existing wardrobe. If yes, you can make it work by practising showing up when nobody is looking. I used to do this all the time. Try out new things on days when you know you are not leaving the house. This is the easiest way to get comfortable with pushing your style options. As you become comfortable with that, push yourself a little further. This is a habit that can move you in any direction you want to go.

Lie #6
I need my husband's / sister's / daughter's approval . . .

Somebody else's approval should not be your number one concern when it comes to your individual style. When you are well connected to who you are and what you like, you can break away from the need to constantly seek approval from other people. Why would you want to give the power to decide who you are to others? That's not to say that you will never ask them what they think. But their opinions should be the icing, not the whole cake. Also, remember that our kids sometimes like to see us in a certain way (old), but that's not necessarily how we see or want to see ourselves!

"Wear the things that you love all the time and inspire yourself every day."

Lie #7
I can't afford / justify it . . .

This is usually something I hear from people who are not in the habit of valuing themselves enough, and it's not always in relation to expensive pieces. However, as you have got this far in the book, I am hoping this is not you. When you stop impulse buying and start to be more strategic about both your wardrobe and the things you want to wear every day to empower yourself, you will see that the things you love are an investment in you.

Always stop and calculate the value per wear. For example, if you choose well when buying a coat or a jacket, you will be able to wear it with many different outfits for several years. This way, you can justify buying something that you love and will be reminded every time you wear it that you are worth it.

Lie #8
I'm not cool enough . . .

What is cool? Think about it. Is it really about what somebody is wearing, or is it the way they are wearing it? Cool is an attitude. It is a vibe that you get from somebody who is confident and happy in their own skin. Everything they do rocks because they believe that they rock. They rock everything that they do, not just their style, and you can too!

If you think you are not cool and you want to be, make it your mission to evolve into someone who is. It might take a little time; you won't make changes overnight. Add a bit of attitude to your style, something that feels like a little stretch but doesn't make you self-conscious. Know who you are and practise being confident in your opinions, one small decision at a time. Keep your eye on the goal, and walk into the future version of you one step at a time. There is nothing like it to help you avoid becoming invisible as you grow older. Some of the coolest women I know are over seventy!

Lie #9
I have too much black . . .

I just might have way too many words to write on this one! "I have too much black." Says who? If you love black and you have a whole wardrobe of it that mixes and matches, way to go! When you are shopping for something new and it fits in with lots of other things that you have, that is the dream as it will expand your existing outfits options. When it comes to buying black for an occasion, it is a no-brainer, as you can wear it for many different occasions and just accessorize it in different ways for each one. Job done!

It is a good idea on days when you are feeling tired to have pops of colour to soften the black, especially close to your face. This can be done with accessories, jewellery, or scarves.

If you are somebody who wears black all the time, you proba-bly have people in your life who try to convince you to switch it for colour. Only cave if it is something that you are interested in trying; do not be railroaded. If you want to inject some colour into your closet, a great way to do that is with accessories and makeup.

CHAPTER 30

YOUR WARDROBE-BUILDING FORMULA

~ ❖ ~

*"Learn the rules like a pro so you can
break them like an artist."*

– PABLO PICASSO

Let's explore a few different ways of curating your wardrobe. Although there is some crossover between all of these methods, each has its signature traits. Some may appeal to you more than others.

Whether you choose one or a combination of more than one way, there are no hard and fast rules. I just want to give you a few guidelines to help you make more informed choices.

I've combined elements of all of these wardrobe types when designing my collections, but I have always stayed focused on ensuring that they are timeless. Steal my strategies. Use them to make your wardrobe timeless so the pieces you invest in serve you not for years but for decades.

The Timeless Wardrobe

Wardrobe style signature

Pieces that do not date. They will look as good in ten years' time as they did on the day you bought them.

What is a timeless wardrobe?

Disagreements exist about what defines a timeless wardrobe. While some insist it hinges on adhering to a specific checklist, I disagree. My view of true timelessness arises from first-hand experience gained over three decades of working with customers. It's about pieces bought years ago, like those from my earliest collections, that are still cherished and worn today, often passed down to the next generation. This goes beyond the typical timeless checklist, transcending items like trench coats and pencil skirts.

Being timeless doesn't mean settling for dull, forgettable attire. It means avoiding the fleeting trends that become obsolete in six months. When you have a genuine emotional connection with a garment, that love remains over the years, especially if you reinvent it. Creating a timeless wardrobe in this manner is inspiring and boosts your confidence, resonating in all aspects of life.

Prioritise flattering cuts and create go-to outfits where simplicity shines. Seek out pieces with unique cuts or details, mixing statement items with well-cut, quality basics. Invest in outerwear, even if it stretches your budget initially, as the cost per wear over time becomes minimal. Your collection will become uniquely yours, a source of wardrobe envy for others.

However, this isn't achievable with cheap, poorly made clothing. An investment in quality pieces reaps empowerment and enduring value. Select pieces that evoke rarity, excitement, curiosity, and emotion. Keep an eye on the future instead of dwelling in the past; avoid becoming a fashion timestamp. Evolve by cherry-picking trends each season.

Building a timeless wardrobe might require a transition. Begin by analysing your existing wardrobe, gradually phasing out highly trend-driven pieces over a couple of seasons. You can sell them to fund new timeless additions.

A timeless wardrobe discourages quick fixes, enabling you to buy less and invest in beloved pieces. You'll find justification for that long-desired handbag or fabulous coat, knowing they'll remain relevant year after year.

By following this path, you'll continue to cherish your timeless pieces a decade or two from now, relishing their enduring appeal.

"I have a raincoat that is nineteen years old. Every time I wear it, people still compliment me. I have many pieces I invested in over the last three decades. My daughters are wearing them now!"

– HELEN MARTIN, STYLIST

The Lifestyle Wardrobe

Wardrobe style signature

Groups of outfits created by strategically planning around the wearer's everyday life.

What is a lifestyle wardrobe?

Many have heard the phrase "Everyone has a lifestyle wardrobe," and indeed, that's true. However, not everyone possesses a thoughtfully planned lifestyle wardrobe. While shopping for special occasions can be enjoyable, it can also lead to an unbalanced wardrobe. You might accumulate numerous items for outings and events while finding your everyday wear section lacking and uninspiring. The goal is to maintain a well-rounded wardrobe that caters to your daily needs.

This strategic wardrobe approach is particularly beneficial for those with hectic lives. Whether you're a business owner, a frequent traveller, or a parent raising a young family, you'll have various boxes to check to ensure you're prepared for every situation. I recall a moment in my life as a newly single mother when I realised my wardrobe needed an adjustment. It had to become more practical and easier to maintain. This realisation prompted the introduction of jerseys into my collection, allowing me to stay well dressed while accommodating the physical demands of my lifestyle. I understood that if I faced this challenge, others did too.

In the midst of a chaotic life, it's easy to fall into a rut. Your personal identity can quickly fade when jeans and a hoodie become your daily uniform. When you're constantly tending to others' needs, particularly while raising a young family, it's easy to lose sight of yourself without even realising it.

In my research, I stumbled upon a concept called "unclothed cognition," which relates to how clothing can impact one's feelings. An interesting study in the *Journal of Experimental Social Psychology* revealed that people's attention increased when they were asked to wear a white coat described as a doctor's lab coat. Intriguingly, the same effect didn't occur when they were told it was a painter's coat.

This is pertinent to our everyday attire because the clothes we choose influence how the world perceives us, subsequently affecting our self-esteem. Therefore, it's vital not to become invisible through our daily clothing choices. Paying attention to your daily attire can positively influence your overall outlook. Feeling good boosts your energy, benefiting not only you but also those around you.

"I have a new motto inspired by Bronagh, my stylist, who said we should never save our best looks for good wear, we should rock them and inspire ourselves every day!"

– OBI JAMES, LEADERSHIP COACH

The Ageless Wardrobe

Wardrobe style signature

Non-conforming style that exudes attitude and the ever-evolving essence of the wearer.

What is an ageless wardrobe?

This wardrobe-building strategy may particularly resonate with those who've reached a certain age. Fortunately, the conversation around aging is evolving, albeit slowly. Having crossed the threshold into the "wrong" side of fifty, I can confidently attest to the magical transformation that occurs. With age comes the liberating realisation that you've earned the right to not give a toss about others' opinions.

The wisdom that accompanies aging is a precious gift, one that should triumph over any desire to appear younger. Embrace what is authentically you and rock it!

As you move through your fifties, chances are you've completed the chapter of raising your children. While this transition can be a bit daunting, don't dwell on it for long, because the most exciting times are right ahead if you choose to seize them. It's a moment to explore all the dreams and aspirations you may have deferred while nurturing your family. There's a whole new lifetime ahead, and it's exhilarating to realise that you hold the brush to paint its canvas. Embrace the future, experiment with new pursuits, learn, create, and consider starting a new career, or even a business venture. These endeavours will keep you vibrant and ever evolving.

Don't allow yourself to slip into the clichéd middle-age stereotype or settle for "granny shoes." Let your wardrobe mirror your unique personality and the wisdom you've earned over the years. Embrace the thrill of trying new things, and let go of worries about the changes that come naturally with age. Focus on maintaining your health rather than chasing youth. Energy is your ally, and it radiates positivity. Keep seeking those timeless pieces that excite you, and enjoy the process.

Learn the art of camouflaging the aspects you'd rather not highlight, and continually assess your evolving body type. Opt for pieces that defy categorisation by age. You could be forty, you could be seventy–it doesn't matter. You understand and embrace sensible guidelines that prevent you from looking out of touch, while never conforming to society's narrow perceptions of age.

"I don't want to dress like my daughter, and I don't want to dress like my mother. My body shape has changed, and I choose pieces that allow me to not focus on that fact. I work with the body shape that I have and pay attention to my assets. Confidence and well-being are the accessories I wear every day."

– BRID FALLON, HOTELIER

The Secret of Layering

Wardrobe style signature

A versatile wardrobe of individual pieces that can be mixed and matched and worn in combinations of layers.

What is the layered wardrobe?

Layering has been a fashion practice spanning centuries, from ancient cavewomen donning animal skins to historical eras where dresses layered over corsets were in vogue. Fortunately, modern-day layering is far more practical and comfortable.

The versatility of layering knows no climate bounds. In colder regions, two thin layers trump one heavier one, thanks to the trapped insulating air in between. Additionally, layers efficiently wick away sweat and shield against rain and wind. In warmer climes, lightweight outer layers paired with inner base layers provide protection from the sun's ultraviolet rays.

Sports brands widely employ layering, leveraging technical fabrics designed for various purposes, from fitted base layers for peak performance to insulating layers for warmth and protective outer shell layers.

In everyday fashion, especially for casual wear, most people are accustomed to layering outfits. It's a skill many of us possess: taking a pair of jeans and a shirt and elevating them with added layers, such as sweaters, jackets, scarves, and more.

However, there's a less common aspect of layering that my brand has honed into an art form over the years. Our jerseys are designed to mix and match seamlessly for everyday wear. This innovation allows for reimagining entire outfits simply by introducing a single new piece. You can also transform an everyday ensemble into something special for occasions by incorporating base jersey layers with statement outer layers, which means that each time you introduce one new piece, you expand your outfit options.

Moreover, layering emerges as a saving grace during one specific life stage–menopause. When your body's temperature fluctuations run wild, lighter layers that you can easily add or shed become your closest allies, offering comfort and control.

"I started layering with a few basic jersey pieces. Each season I add one or two pieces to my collection. Because I can mix and match the colours, my outfit choices multiply each time!"

– CLAIRE GOLDEN, STYLIST

The Capsule Wardrobe

Wardrobe style signature

A minimal wardrobe of pieces chosen to mix and match together in which less frivolous and more mindful options are prioritised.

What is the capsule wardrobe?

The concept of capsule wardrobes, though much discussed in recent years, is far from novel. Susie Faux, the proprietor of London's Wardrobe boutique, coined the term back in the 1970s.

At its core, a capsule wardrobe is about living with fewer clothes, a practice that extends beyond your closet to declutter your life and, by extension, your mind.

An easy litmus test to gauge if this approach aligns with you is to clear your desk or kitchen countertops completely. Only return the essentials. For your desk, this might entail a candle, a vase of flowers, a notebook, a nice pen, and perhaps your laptop. For the kitchen, keep only the kettle and, again, a candle or vase of flowers. How does this make you feel? If the newfound space sparks inspiration rather than anxiety, a capsule wardrobe could offer the same sense of liberation in your daily life.

This is my chosen wardrobe strategy, and I can attest that living with fewer clothes clears mental clutter. I half-jokingly claim that I prefer to keep my head "empty," but it's not mere jest. A clear mind invites the good stuff to flourish, from inspiration and mindfulness to savouring life's simple pleasures and continuous learning.

In my exploration of various online articles on capsule wardrobes, I encountered an eye-roll-inducing trend. Many people shared stories of trying and failing to adhere to set rules regarding the number of items and their prescribed types. Wardrobe management should be enjoyable, and imposing rigid constraints misses the point.

So here's the crux of it: embrace the idea of a capsule wardrobe but toss out the rulebook. Better yet, pen your own guidelines. Discard two common rules: that you must have a fixed number of items and that a predetermined list should dictate your choices.

In your own capsule, set your own terms. Allow as many pieces as you find appropriate and let the items be precisely what you desire. The key lies in ensuring that each new addition complements your existing wardrobe, expanding your outfit possibilities. Your collection can consist of versatile basics in neutral tones that harmonise seamlessly or statement pieces that creatively mix with simpler elements. My own capsule wardrobe includes mix and match jersey pieces combined with pinnies, dungarees, oversized shirts, jeans, jackets, and coats that I have collected over the years. My jersey pieces also form a base for more occasion wear outfits which are completed by adding signature over pieces that are brought out year after year.

Stay true to your style; don't yield to others' expectations. If you sense resistance, stand firm in the knowledge that people encounter the best version of you when you stay authentic, and they'll quickly catch on.

"I have built up my wardrobe over many years. I never get rid of my pieces; I still love them all. Each new purchase not only moves my wardrobe on, it creates several new outfit options which are unique to me."

– MARY MASTERSON, PUBLICAN

CHAPTER 31

THE CURATE
FRAMEWORK

Your Closet-Curating Companion

Instead of handing you an instruction manual, I'm gifting
you a memorable framework, your guiding companion for
curating your closet and making the most of your shopping
experiences.

It's designed to keep you focused, helping you make mindful
choices as you refine your personal style. Each step is a key to
unlocking and elevating your outfit potential and showing up
as the most empowered version of you every day.

C – Collect

Collect more of what makes you feel great.

Identify the things you already own that make you feel amazing when you wear them. Reflect on why you feel this way so your reasons can inform future choices. Make it your wardrobe purpose to build around pieces that empower you every day and remind you that you are worth investing in.

U – Unleash

Unleash your inner goddess.

Unleash who you authentically are and show up unapologetically. There is a perfect version of you for every occasion. Curate your closet using the mindsets of your archetype toolkit so you show up feeling confident and ready to take on the world.

R – Refine

Refine how you shop.

Make a shopping list and keep it on your phone. Everything that you are missing or that potentially expands your outfit options goes on the list. Use it whenever you feel like a treat. Stay focused and eliminate impulse buys that do not serve you well.

A – Align

Align future purchases to your authentic identity.

Be the gatekeeper of your closet. Nothing makes it in there that isn't aligned with who you are and how you want to show up. Nothing gets in there that hasn't earned its place. Always look at a potential purchase through the lens of how it expands your outfit options. If it requires additional purchases to make it work, leave it behind.

T – Transform

Transform what you already have.

Take outfits from previous occasions and tweak them to create outfits for future occasions. Have these on standby so occasions do not prompt buying trips. This will save your clothing budget for timeless items that will serve you for many years.

E – Evolve

Evolve effortlessly over time.

This is my number one tip for ensuring that you never get stuck in a rut. Evolve with intention every season. Curate your closet every season for the season ahead. The reward will not just be a closet that inspires you when you throw open the doors each morning. The work you do will keep you evolving in every area of life.

Your CURATE framework is your trusted companion on this style journey, empowering you to curate your closet with purpose, elegance, and intention.

CHAPTER 32

TRANSFORMATION BEYOND THE CLOSET

The Ripple Effect of an Empowered Wardrobe

Your empowered wardrobe isn't confined to your closet; it ripples into every aspect of your life. As you embody the mindsets of your archetypes, you'll notice a shift in how you perceive yourself and how others perceive you. The confidence and authenticity you radiate through your style extend far beyond fashion–they become integral parts of your identity.

Gaining self-assurance in various life domains

Remember, your archetypes aren't just about what you wear; they're about how you show up in the world. With your archetype toolkit in hand, you'll find that self-assurance comes more naturally. The self-assured Creative, the poised Sophisticate, or the empowered Provider–each archetype contributes to your overall self-confidence. As you tap into these different mindsets, you'll discover a newfound assertiveness in your personal and professional interactions.

Navigating challenges with a newfound sense of self

Life is a journey of ups and downs, challenges and triumphs. With your archetype toolkit, you're equipped to face these moments with resilience and authenticity, stepping out of your bedroom each morning ready to take on the day.

The Trail Blazer's daring spirit, the Romantic's vulnerability, and the Athlete's determination–these attributes guide you through obstacles and help you navigate uncharted territories. Your style is a visual representation of your inner strength, reminding you that you can overcome anything life throws your way.

The power of owning your narrative

Your empowered style is a powerful narrative that you craft every day. It speaks of your growth, your resilience, and your journey towards self-discovery. Your style archetypes offer a language that resonates with your soul, helping you articulate who you are without saying a word. By consistently choosing outfits that align with your archetypes, you're solidifying your commitment to authenticity and empowerment.

Embracing your ongoing transformation

The journey of embracing your style archetypes is ongoing. Just as you evolve and grow, your style evolves with you. Be open to experimenting, to trying new combinations, and to embracing new archetypes that resonate with your changing self. This is a lifelong adventure of self-discovery, empowerment, and self-expression. The transformation you've initiated by delving into your archetypes will continue to unfold, guiding you towards greater self-awareness and a more authentic life.

Remember that your style is a reflection of your inner essence, a celebration of your journey, and a source of empowerment. The archetypes are your companions on this path, helping you navigate the complexities of life with confidence and grace.

~ ❖ ~

"Lurking beneath the surface in every woman is a goddess. Wake her up. Let her come out to play. She is your soul mate, your best friend, your first and last love. You were born with her and you will die with her. You don't need anyone else's approval."

– MARY GRANT

WHAT'S NEXT

If you enjoyed the book and would like to go deeper into curating your style archetype mindset toolkit, you will love Archetype Alchemy, a self-paced transformation experience.

Visit *www.archetype-alchemy.com* to find out more.

If you want to go deeper, fly higher or move faster towards your life vision while keeping your balance.

I've got you covered.

Pop over to my website : www.marygrant.com to see how we can work together. The best way to contact me is by direct message on Instagram.

 www.marygrant.com

@themarygrant

@MaryGrantCoach

linkedin.com/in/mary-grant-coach

If you would like to see my capsule collections, you can find us at our website below and connect with us on my fashion Instagram page.

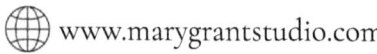 www.marygrantstudio.com

@marygrantstudio

ACKNOWLEDGEMENTS

There are so many people in my life that I am so grateful for who have been there through the good and bad times and without whom I would not be where I am today.

To my kids, Bronagh, Pluto and James. You are and always will be my reason *why*. It doesn't matter what age you are, I will always be mama bear!

To my parents Nora and Mick, who's combined creativity I have to thank for my creative genes. Thank you for always believing me and lovingly challenging me to believe there was nothing I couldn't do.

To my siblings, Gillian, John and Damian, who have had my back all through the tough times. Take one on . . . take them all on!

To my amazing customers. Everything I do in my business is in service to you. I see your faces when I'm designing and creating my coaching programmes. You are my muse, my filter through which designs either make the cut or don't. Your stories have shaped my coaching vision. I see every place in life where you get stuck and held back and it fuels my desire to empower women to evolve effortlessly and chase their dreams while juggling the balls of family life.

To everyone who is or has ever been on my team. There are too many to mention, I don't want to risk leaving anybody out. Know that you had a role to play in my business, not just surviving but thriving for thirty years. I am more grateful to you than you will ever know.

A big thank you to my besties, many of whom have never met each other. You have supported me and kept me going with laughter and shenanigans over the years: Teresa Kelly, Johnny Kelly, Carole Alagna, Siobhan Canning, Clare O'Sullivan, Mary Donoghue, Alison Kelly, Adeline Molloy, Lesley Kavanagh, Yvonne Sourke, Tom Sourke, Johnny McConnell, Barbara Lenihan, Dee Ahearn, Jacqui Boyle, Sheena Lyons, Brid Fallon, Lisa Matthews, Dee Hagan, Clare Johnson, Bernie & Sean Flanagan, we may not see each other often but you are never far from my mind.

A special shout out to my business buddies who kept me going, putting up with my endless requests for feedback on the book and the cover. Lorraine Gannon, Sonja Leeson, Jane Malyon, Obi James, Michelle Sandler, Donna Clarke, Marta Spirk, Cody Burch, Taralyn Jensen,

To my Aligned ladies who read the first draft of the book and gave me invaluable feedback : Alexis Mina, Jo Lalor, Patti Atwood Dial. To Tina McCrossan and Eavan O'Brien who have jumped in and facilitated self care meetings for our community, I will always appreciate that more than you know.

A special shout out to Dianne Cunningham Ellis who is my daily partner in crime, even though we are a continent apart! We challenge each other and move mountains every day despite a 6 hour time difference. I am here for every crazy minute of it.

Thank you so much to my publishing team at The Journey Institute. What an absolute whirlwind after meeting you through my journey with TEDx Cherry Creek. Michael Jenet, Dafna Jenet, you are a dream to work with. Thank you for your guidance and for making everything so light and easy. Thanks also to Jessica Medberry, your edits uplevelled the whole book.

To my illustrators Dhanushika Silva and Anastasiia Asiosi, thank you for taking my vision and turning it into exactly the right images. I am in awe of your talent!

To everybody in the fashion industry and in the press that have supported my journey along the way. I am eternally grateful for your belief in me and supporting me, even when I didn't know where I was going! A special shout out to Shelly Corkery, Nikki Creedon, Jenny Turner, Dorothy Ronan, Louise Flanagan, Kate O'Dwyer, Kate Gaffney, Bernie Flanagan who each held a key that unlocked a standout moment in my 30-year journey. And to Constance Harris, Deirdre McQuillan, Barbara Power, who supported and endorsed my collections over the last 30 years.

Finally, to anybody who has touched my life in any way. I appreciate you. We are a product of our experiences, and every step of the journey has brought me to the top of an amazing mountain. There have been many curveballs sent to test me, but now I know I can take on any mountain . . .

So can you.

ABOUT THE AUTHOR

Mary Grant is a designer and entrepreneur with a career spanning over three decades. Her journey has been one of constant evolution, marked by successful business partnerships, design and business awards and a consistent presence in the press.

With an innate flair for fashion that transcends the ordinary, Mary's designs have graced the wardrobes of celebrities and music icons. Her creativity has taken her on a remarkable business journey, from owning her own brand stores to establishing concessions in prestigious department stores, pop-ups in a luxury outlet village, and partnerships with top-end boutiques worldwide.

Today, Mary's entrepreneurial spirit continues to thrive as she launches capsule collections twice a year through her e-commerce business. This venture is fully aligned with her vision for a lifestyle that balances family, creativity, and success, while allowing time for personal growth and pursuing other passions.

However, Mary's true passion lies in making a meaningful impact in the lives of her clients. She is an accredited coach, specializing in empowering leaders and entrepreneurs to embrace constant evolution, show up powerfully, and create a dynamic path to achieve their highest-level self and their most audacious goals and aspirations. Her story is an invitation to explore the journey of empowerment, unlock your true potential, navigate life's complexities, and build unstoppable momentum towards your life vision.

As a divorced mother of three, Mary was driven not only by her deep desire to provide for her family, but also by her passion for creativity and innovation. Her unique journey is a testament to her resilience and serves as an inspiration for others navigating the challenges of entrepreneurship while staying true to themselves and their families.

Beyond her professional pursuits, Mary enjoys photography, road trips, leisurely beach walks, and the thrill of challenging herself and pushing boundaries for fun.

"Originally from Dublin, Mary lives in Kildare, Ireland, with her three young adult kids, each on their own exciting journey of self-discovery and growth.

Journey Institute Press

Journey Institute Press is a non-profit publishing house created by authors to flip the publishing model for new authors. Created with intention and purpose to provide the highest quality publishing resources available to authors whose stories might otherwise not be told.

JI Press focusses on women, BIPOC, and LGBTQ+ authors without regard to the genre of their work.

As a Publishing House, our goal is to create a supportive, nurturing, and encouraging environment that puts the author above the publisher in the publishing model.

Journey Ink Publishing is an Imprint of Journey Institute Press, a Division of 50 in 52 Journey, Inc.